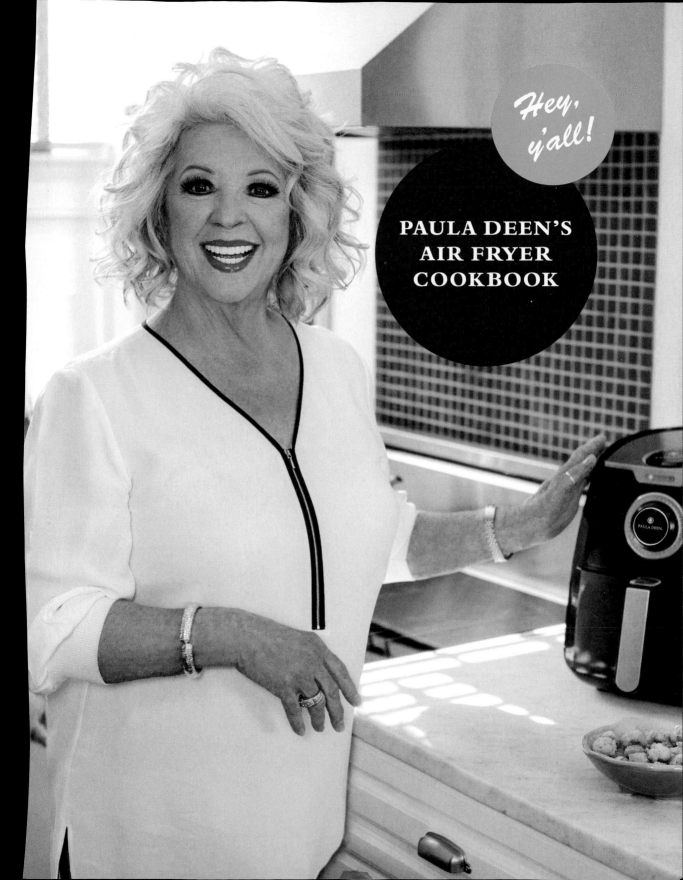

Hey, y'all!

PAULA DEEN'S AIR FRYER COOKBOOK

PAULA DEEN'S AIR FRYER COOKBOOK

Paula Deen

 Paula Deen Ventures
2391 Downing Ave.
Thunderbolt, GA 31404

Library of Congress Cataloging-in-Publication data is available.

ISBN 978-1-943016-07-5

Paula Deen Ventures and colophon are
registered trademarks of Paula Deen Ventures, Inc.

PRODUCED BY WILSTED & TAYLOR PUBLISHING SERVICES
Production manager Christine Taylor
Copy editor Lynn Meinhardt
Designer and compositor Nancy Koerner
Proofreader Jennifer Brown
Printer's devil Lillian Wilsted

Manufactured in the United States of America

21 20 19 18   10 9 8 7

CONTENTS

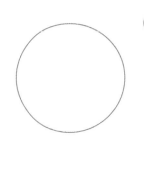

③ BEEF/PORK/VEAL

④ SEAFOOD

⑤ SIDES

⑥ AN ODE TO THE POTATO

⑦ SWEETS

PREFACE

I'm a Southern cook, and it is no secret that I love fried foods. Of course, my restaurants all have deep fryers, but I even have a big old deep fryer in my home. Turning on the deep fryer, waiting for it to heat up, and smelling hot oil in the air was a ritual. My arms became immune to the little kisses the oil burned on my skin. It was all worth it to bite into the delicious, crispy perfection deep-frying delivered.

Being healthy is of utmost importance, but being healthy *and* happy—that's a bonus. We all crave to be around our loved ones as long as possible. I want my grandbabies to grow up watching me in the kitchen the way I watched my Grandma Paul in her kitchen. I just loved spending hours with Grandma as she cooked the best fried chicken in her cast-iron skillet with just the right amount of oil, buttermilk biscuits slathered with butter that melted in your mouth, and her grits—honey, they were a gift from the food gods.

I have maintained a forty-pound weight loss for four years, and I have done so while continuing to eat my favorite Southern foods. I spent months in the kitchen creating healthier versions of my classic recipes for my book *Paula Deen Cuts the Fat*, and I was able to lighten up recipes and practice moderation. But a key ingredient to any recipe is how you cook your food. As much as I love my deep fryer, I knew it could no longer be my best friend.

When air-frying was introduced to me, I admit I was skeptical. What about the crispy crunch I loved so much? Working to develop the Paula Deen Air Fryer, I learned that I could literally have my cake and eat it too. Guess what, y'all? I now have a new best friend—the Paula Deen Air Fryer. I never could have imagined all the tastiness this countertop appliance could create. I became determined to convert my recipes for the air fryer. My friend Deb Murray and I have the same love and passion for food and for sharing. It was only natural that I would turn to her to assist me with adapting my recipes for this wonderful new air fryer. Many thanks to

Laurie Bain the prep queen and Yildred Lamb for her beautiful photography. I feel like the recipes (and the fryer) can change your life. I really do!

We had a lot of fun, but it was hard work to narrow down the recipes to 150. If you can cook a dish in your oven, on top of your stove, on a grill, or in a microwave, you can cook it in this air fryer. You will be amazed that a three-pound chicken or half a turkey breast can fit in this air fryer. The Fried Pecan–Bourbon Glaze (page 51) is the perfect topper, but the turkey breast alone is moist and delicious. There's no need to wait for Thanksgiving, y'all. Oh, did I forget to mention? Air-frying it only takes 30 minutes, friends.

The Salmon Burgers (page 95) are so scrumptious you forget how healthy they are. Speaking of healthy, hurrah for the Brussels sprout. As far as I am concerned, this vegetable cannot receive enough accolades, and I think you will love the Roasted Brussels Sprouts with Lemon Zest (page 121). Or doctor up the morsel any way you want. The Fried Apple Pies (page 175) you can make as healthy or as decadent as you choose.

If you know me, you know how I adore a potato. This book would not be complete without an ode to the potato—a full chapter is dedicated to my love. I've deconstructed the sweet potato with my recipe for Sweet Potato Fries with Marshmallows (page 153). Let your imagination run wild with appetizers, y'all, but I'm here to tell you that the Mashed Potato Egg Rolls (page 162) are a great start.

You don't have to use a Paula Deen Air Fryer (but it is the best—I'm just saying). The recipes in this book will work with any air fryer, though you may need to adjust temperatures and cooking times.

Love and best air-fried dishes,

AIR-FRYING TIPS

Hey, y'all. I have been testing recipes and experimenting with my air fryer, and I want to share my discoveries. First, let me tell ya, I love my peach-colored Paula Deen Air Fryer. The color beautifully complements the copper in my kitchen. My air fryer sits on my kitchen counter plugged directly into the outlet.

Second, here are two important tips on usage: do not place anything on top of the appliance, and let the appliance cool down half an hour before cleaning. Then just rinse it off—easy.

The best tip I can share is to read your air fryer instructions before using the appliance. Once you have read the instructions, you can have fun air-frying all of my delicious recipes.

Keep in mind that temperatures and cooking times are guidelines, so use your judgment to determine when food is done. Cooking times will vary, depending on the size of your air fryer and your food. For example, when you or I bake apples, you don't know how large my apples are, and I don't know how large your apples are, so my recipe's cooking time is only a guide. Open the basket, look at the apples, and stick them with a toothpick to determine if they are cooked through. The easily removed air fryer basket allows you look in on the apples, shake the basket, and pop it back into the air fryer to continue cooking if need be.

Here are a few more bits of advice to help you enjoy your air fryer.

- Do not add oil to the fryer. Only apply oil to the food being cooked in the air fryer.

- I recommend purchasing an oil mister, and, of course, the Paula Deen Oil Mister is the best. I have several, each filled with a different oil—coconut, avocado, and grapeseed. I chose the oil that best complements the food I am cooking.

- I spray food as it cooks, and I like to say, "Give the food a little kiss of oil."

- I love to use sea salt—kiss a potato recipe with avocado oil from your mister, shake on sea salt, and your tongue will slap your mouth, it's so delicious!

- You can cook without oil, but to get a true crispy fried coating, the food should be kissed.

- When using a flour-coated recipe, mist with oil once (fantastic); add two more misty kisses, and you are in crispy-crunchy "deep-fried" heaven.

- Choose coatings to go with your lifestyle. If you are cooking paleo, use ground almonds for the coating; if cooking Atkins, use ground pork rinds; if cooking gluten-free, use quinoa; or feel free to just go naked, without any coating at all.

- Do not overcrowd the basket—the air fryer cooks so quickly that less is better and will produce a balance between crunch and moistness. Work in batches, and just reload the basket when each batch is done.

- Use uniform cuts when you slice or dice meat and veggies—not too fat, not too skinny—just simple, consistent portions.

- If I want pure perfection when air-frying food coated with flour or panko breadcrumbs, I shake off the excess coating and chill the food 15 to 20 minutes before air-frying.

- When baking in your air fryer, it's best to preheat the air fryer for 5 to 10 minutes: definitely preheat when preparing cookies, cakes, and donuts. Preheating is not necessary for all other foods.

- Air-frying does a great job of air-*steaming*. You can take any veggie, cut it up into equal-size pieces, and steam it to perfection.

- When air-frying foods with fat that will melt away—steak, chicken with skin on, and bacon—randomly check the basket during cooking and pour off excess fat.

- I recommend shaking the basket instead of turning over the food. While I shake the basket, I shake my hips to get a little exercise. Add some music and strobe lights and have an air fryer party. The perfect recipe for this party is my Disco Fries, on page 145.

- You don't always need a recipe. The air fryer is great for reheating pizza and frozen snacks and making toast in the morning. Create your own recipes.

- The air fryer may look like an adult Easy-Bake Oven, but this, my friends, is no toy. With adult supervision, the air fryer is a wonderful tool with which to teach children to cook. There are no open flames, and the timer can be set to perfectly cook food at just the right temperature. I so enjoy making air-fried cookies with my granboys, almost as much as I love eating those cookies.

PAULA'S FAVORITES

Pigs in a Blanket • 10

*Bacon-Wrapped
Cheese-Filled Jalapeños • 6*

Brie en Croûte • 20

FRIED CHEESE STICKS

Serves 6

12	part-skim mozzarella cheese sticks
¼ cup	cornstarch
2	large eggs
2 cups	Italian-seasoned breadcrumbs
¼ cup	grated Parmesan cheese
	oil, for spraying
	marinara sauce, for dipping

1. Separate cheese sticks and freeze for 2 hours.

2. Place cornstarch in a large plastic bag. In a medium bowl, beat eggs. In a shallow dish or pie pan, combine breadcrumbs and Parmesan cheese. Place frozen cheese sticks in bag with cornstarch and shake. Remove one cheese stick and dip in beaten egg, shaking off any excess. Press into breadcrumb mixture and place on baking sheet lined with parchment paper. Repeat with remaining cheese sticks. Spray cheese sticks well with oil.

3. Working in batches of 6, place cheese sticks in air fryer basket. Do not overcrowd. Set temperature to 400 degrees. Air fry for 7 minutes, shaking basket frequently during cooking. Turn cheese sticks, and air fry for 3 minutes more. Repeat with remaining cheese sticks. Serve with warm marinara sauce on the side.

AIR-FRIED
MAC AND CHEESE SQUARES

Serves 6

1 pound	elbow macaroni
1 cup	milk
4 tablespoons (½ stick)	butter, cut into pieces
½ teaspoon	salt
½ teaspoon	pepper
½ cup	sour cream
2 cups	grated Cheddar cheese
	flour, for dredging
4	large eggs
3 cups	breadcrumbs
	oil, for spraying

1   Cook macaroni according to package directions. Drain, rinse in cold water, and drain again. Cool for several minutes. In a Dutch oven, warm milk and butter over medium heat until butter is melted. Stir in salt and pepper. Whisk in sour cream until smooth, then add Cheddar cheese, stirring until melted and smooth. Add macaroni and blend. Pour pasta mixture into a shallow rectangular baking dish and chill for at least 2 hours.

2   Cut macaroni and cheese into squares. Place flour in a shallow dish. In a shallow bowl, beat eggs. Place breadcrumbs in another shallow dish. Take each square and dredge in flour, dip in egg, then dredge in breadcrumbs. Coat well. Place squares on a baking sheet lined with parchment paper. Spray tops of squares with oil.

3   Working in batches of 6 to 8, place squares in air fryer basket. Do not overcrowd. Set temperature to 400 degrees, and air fry for 5 minutes. Turn squares, spray with oil, and air fry for 5 minutes more. Remove squares to a serving platter. Repeat with remaining squares. Serve warm.

FRIED GREEN TOMATOES
with VIDALIA ONION RELISH

Serves 4

2	white onions, diced
½ cup	mayonnaise
½ cup	rice wine vinegar
2 tablespoons	brown sugar
2 tablespoons	fresh chives, chopped
1	large firm green tomato
	salt
1 cup	buttermilk
1 cup	all-purpose flour
	black pepper to taste
	oil, for spraying

1. For the relish, in a medium bowl, mix onions, mayonnaise, rice wine vinegar, brown sugar, and chives. Cover with plastic wrap and marinade for at least 2 hours.

2. For the fried tomatoes, using a mandoline, cut tomato into ¼-inch-thick slices. Lay tomato slices in a shallow pan and sprinkle with salt. Place tomato slices in a colander and allow time for salt to pull out water, approximately 30 minutes. Place buttermilk in a shallow bowl. In a shallow dish, mix flour and pepper. Dip tomatoes in buttermilk, then dredge in flour mixture.

3. Line air fryer basket with parchment paper. Working in batches of 4, spray both sides of tomato slices with oil and place in air fryer basket. Set temperature to 400 degrees, and air fry for 5 minutes. Turn slices, spray with oil, and air fry for 5 minutes more. Set aside tomato slices and keep warm. Repeat with remaining tomato slices. Serve hot with relish on the side.

BACON-WRAPPED CHEESE-FILLED JALAPEÑOS

Serves 4

8	jalapeño peppers, whole
¼ cup	Cheddar or Boursin cheese spread
8 strips	thin bacon
	oil, for spraying

1. Place jalapeño peppers in air fryer basket. Set temperature to 400 degrees. Cook for 4 minutes. Let peppers sit in air fryer for 5 minutes. Remove peppers from basket, peel off loosened skins, then slice each pepper in half lengthwise. With a sharp knife, remove membranes and seeds and rinse well. Pat dry with paper towels.

2. Fill each half pepper with one teaspoon or more of cheese spread and wrap with bacon strip. Secure bacon with toothpick.

3. Working in batches of 6, spray stuffed peppers with oil and place in air fryer basket. Set temperature to 400 degrees, and air fry for 5 minutes. Turn peppers, spray with oil, and air fry for 4 minutes more, or until bacon is desired doneness. Repeat with remaining peppers.

Hot and cheesy— just pop them in your mouth!

FRIED DILL PICKLES

Serves 18

one 24-ounce jar	kosher dill pickle spears or slices
1 teaspoon	garlic powder
½ cup	The Lady & Sons Signature Hot Sauce
½ cup	buttermilk
1¾ cups	self-rising flour
¼ cup	self-rising white cornmeal
1 teaspoon	salt
½ teaspoon	pepper
	oil, for spraying

1. Drain juice from pickle jar, leaving pickles in place. To the jar, add garlic powder, The Lady & Sons Signature Hot Sauce, and buttermilk. Marinade pickles for 30 minutes. In a medium bowl, combine flour, cornmeal, salt, and pepper and mix well.

2. Dredge each pickle in flour mixture, spray with oil, and lay on baking tray lined with parchment paper. Refrigerate pickles for at least 15 minutes.

3. Spray each pickle again with oil. In batches of 6, place pickles in air fryer basket. Set temperature to 400 degrees, and air fry for 5 minutes. Turn pickles, and air fry for 5 minutes more. Repeat with remaining pickles.

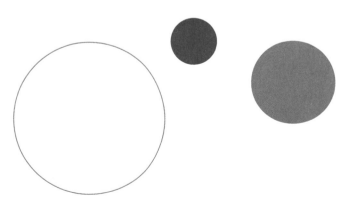

CRUNCHY ONION RINGS *with* CHIPOTLE CREAM DIPPING SAUCE

Serves 4 to 6

1 cup	buttermilk
1	large egg
1 sleeve	soda crackers, crushed
1 cup	all-purpose flour
1 teaspoon	salt
⅛ teaspoon	cayenne pepper
2	large onions, sliced ¼ inch thick and separated into rings
	oil, for spraying

1 In a shallow dish, whisk together buttermilk and egg. In another shallow dish, combine crushed crackers, flour, salt, and cayenne pepper. Dip onion rings in buttermilk mixture, shaking off any excess, then dredge in cracker mixture. Place onion rings on a baking sheet lined with parchment paper, cover with plastic wrap, and refrigerate for 30 minutes.

2 Working in batches, spray onion rings with oil and place in air fryer basket in a single layer. Do not overcrowd. Set temperature to 400 degrees, and air fry for 2 minutes. Without turning onion rings, spray with oil and air fry for 3 minutes more. Turn onion rings, spray with oil, and air fry for 3 minutes longer. Remove onion rings to a serving bowl and keep warm. Repeat with remaining onion rings. Serve warm with *Chipotle Cream Dipping Sauce.*

Chipotle Cream Dipping Sauce

one 8-ounce container sour cream
½ chipotle pepper, canned in adobo sauce, minced
½ teaspoon adobo sauce from can
1 tablespoon heavy whipping cream
2 teaspoons fresh lime juice
½ teaspoon chili powder

In a small bowl, combine sour cream, chipotle pepper, adobo sauce, whipping cream, lime juice, and chili powder. Cover and refrigerate until ready to serve.

Makes 1 cup

FRIED TORTILLA CHIPS

Serves 2

4 fresh corn tortillas

oil, for spraying

Paula Deen's House Seasoning (see page 40) to taste

1 On a cutting board, stack tortillas and cut into 6 equal wedges. Spray tortilla wedges on both sides with oil and place in air fryer basket. Set temperature to 400 degrees, and air fry for 10 minutes, shaking basket occasionally.

2 Sprinkle chips with House Seasoning, cool, and store in an airtight container.

PIGS IN A BLANKET

Serves 4

one 12-ounce can refrigerated crescent dough

4 frankfurters

oil, for spraying

ketchup, for serving

mustard, for serving

1 On a flat surface, separate dough into 8 triangles. Cut each frankfurter in half crosswise. Place one frankfurter half on wide end of each dough triangle and roll up.

2 Working in batches of 4, spray each wrapped frankfurter with oil and place in air fryer basket lined in parchment paper. Set temperature to 375 degrees, and air fry for 5 minutes. Turn frankfurters, spray with oil, and air fry for 3 minutes more, or until golden brown. Repeat with remaining frankfurters. Serve warm with ketchup and mustard.

BUFFALO CHICKEN PINWHEELS

Serves 8

2 cups	shredded deli rotisserie chicken
2 ounces	cream cheese, softened
2 ounces	crumbled blue cheese, softened
2 tablespoons	Louisiana hot sauce
¾ cup	shredded Cheddar cheese
one 8-ounce can	refrigerated crescent dough
	oil, for spraying

1. In a medium bowl, combine chicken, cream cheese, blue cheese, Louisiana hot sauce, and Cheddar cheese.

2. On a lightly floured surface, spread out crescent dough, and pinch interior seams closed. Spread dough evenly with chicken mixture, leaving ¼-inch border on all sides. Roll jelly-roll style and pinch seam to seal. Place seam side down, and slice into 8 pinwheels.

3. Line air fryer basket with parchment paper. Working in batches of 4, spray each pinwheel with oil on both sides and place, cut side down, in air fryer basket in a single layer. Set temperature to 350 degrees, and air fry for 12 minutes. Turn and spray with oil halfway through cooking. Repeat with remaining pinwheels. Serve warm.

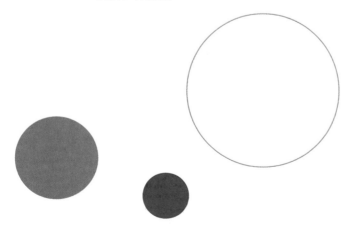

FRIED RAVIOLI ON A STICK

Serves 4

1 cup	all-purpose flour
2	eggs
1 cup	breadcrumbs
½ cup	grated Parmesan cheese, plus more, for sprinkling
2 tablespoons	dried oregano
1 tablespoon	dried thyme
3 teaspoons	Paula Deen's House Seasoning (see page 40)
12	frozen ravioli, thawed
	oil, for spraying
½ cup	pesto, for dipping

1. Place flour in a medium bowl. In a small bowl, beat eggs. In a shallow dish, mix breadcrumbs, ½ cup of the Parmesan cheese, oregano, thyme, and House Seasoning.

2. Add ravioli to flour, toss to coat, and gently shake off excess. Dip each ravioli in egg, shaking off excess. Roll each ravioli gently in breadcrumb mixture. On a skewer, thread 3 breaded ravioli. Spray both sides with oil.

3. Working in batches of 4, place skewers in air fryer basket. Set temperature to 400 degrees, and air fry for 4 minutes. Turn skewers, spray with oil, and air fry for 2 minutes more. Repeat with remaining skewers. Sprinkle with Parmesan cheese, and serve warm with warm pesto on the side.

ROASTED GARLIC FOCACCIA

Serves 4

1¼ cups	warm water (105 to 115 degrees)	3 tablespoons	olive oil
one ¼-ounce package	active dry yeast	2 heads	garlic
			oil, for spraying
2 teaspoons	sugar		cornmeal, for sprinkling
3½ cups	all-purpose flour	2 cups	grated Asiago cheese
1½ teaspoons	salt		fresh basil, thinly sliced, for garnish

1. In a small bowl, combine warm water, yeast, and sugar. Let stand for 5 minutes. In a food processor, combine flour and salt. With processor running, slowly add yeast mixture and olive oil and process until dough forms a ball.

2. Turn dough onto a lightly floured surface and knead until smooth and elastic (about 5 minutes). Place dough in a lightly greased bowl, turning to completely grease. Loosely cover, and let rise in warm place (85 degrees) free from drafts for 1 hour or until doubled in bulk. Punch dough down, and let rest for 10 minutes. On a lightly floured surface, roll dough into two 12-inch-diameter circles.

3. Cut ½ inch off pointed end of garlic, keeping cloves intact. Spray with oil, wrap in foil, and place in air fryer basket. Set temperature to 375 degrees, and air fry for 10 minutes. When cool enough to handle, squeeze garlic pulp into small bowl. Mash garlic with fork and set aside.

4. Place one dough round in air fryer basket and spray with oil. Set temperature to 350 degrees, and air fry for 10 minutes. Remove dough. Spray air fryer basket with oil and sprinkle lightly with cornmeal. Return dough to air fryer basket, and using handle of a wooden spoon, make indentations in top of dough at 1-inch intervals. Spray with oil, spread roasted garlic evenly over dough, and sprinkle dough with Asiago cheese. Raise temperature to 375 degrees, and air fry for 10 minutes more. Repeat with second round of dough. Garnish focaccia with basil before serving.

SAUSAGE AND CHEESE BALLS

Serves 4

1 pound	bulk spicy Italian sausage, room temperature
2 cups	grated sharp Cheddar cheese, room temperature
2 tablespoons	grated Vidalia onion
½ cup	milk
2 cups	baking mix
	kosher salt to taste
	black pepper to taste
	oil, for spraying
½ cup	mayonnaise
2 tablespoons	Dijon mustard
2 tablespoons	honey

1 Combine Italian sausage, Cheddar cheese, onion, milk, baking mix, salt, and pepper in a stand mixer with a paddle attachment and blend for 2 minutes. Form mixture into 1-inch balls.

2 Working in batches of 12, spray each sausage ball with oil and place in air fryer basket. Do not overcrowd. Set temperature to 350 degrees, and air fry for 10 minutes, turning balls halfway through cooking.

3 In a small bowl, combine mayonnaise, mustard, and honey. Serve warm sausage balls with honey-mustard dip on the side.

PORK-SLAW EGG ROLLS

Serves 12

one 2½-pound	boneless Boston butt roast or pork shoulder	⅓ cup	barbecue sauce, plus more, for serving
2 tablespoons	Paula Deen Butt Massage★	1 teaspoon	Paula Deen's House Seasoning (see page 40)
one 16-ounce bag	tri-color coleslaw mix	two 16-ounce packages	egg roll wrappers
¼ cup	diced celery		oil, for spraying
2 tablespoons	sweet pickle relish		

1. Preheat oven to 350 degrees. Line roasting pan with heavy-duty aluminum foil. Place roast in pan and rub with Paula Deen Butt Massage. Cover tightly with foil and bake for 3 hours, or until tender. Let roast cool to touch. Shred pork with a fork. Reserve all but 2½ cups of the shredded pork for another use.

2. In a large bowl, combine 2½ cups of the shredded pork, coleslaw mix, celery, and pickle relish. In a small bowl, combine barbecue sauce and House Seasoning. Pour seasoned barbecue sauce over pork mixture, and toss gently to coat.

3. Place one egg roll wrapper on a flat surface with one corner pointing toward you. Using a pastry brush, lightly brush corners with water. Spoon ⅓ cup of pork filling in center of egg roll wrapper. Fold bottom corner of wrapper over filling. Fold left and right corners over filling. Tightly roll filled end toward remaining corner, pressing gently to seal. Repeat with remaining egg roll wrappers.

4. Working in batches of 4, spray each egg roll with oil and place in air fryer basket. Do not overcrowd. Set temperature to 400 degrees, and air fry for 5 minutes. Turn egg rolls, spray with oil, and air fry for 5 minutes more. Repeat with remaining egg rolls. Serve warm with barbecue sauce.

★ *Butt Massage is a blend of paprika, garlic, and onion powder.*

FRIED BARBECUE MEATBALLS

Serves 6 to 8

2 tablespoons	olive oil
1	onion, finely chopped
2	stalks celery, finely chopped
2	cloves garlic, minced
2 pounds	ground beef
1 pound	ground pork
1 cup	evaporated milk
1 cup	breadcrumbs
2	large eggs
1½ teaspoons	salt
2 teaspoons	chili powder
½ teaspoon	black pepper
	oil, for spraying
1 jar	Paula Deen barbecue sauce

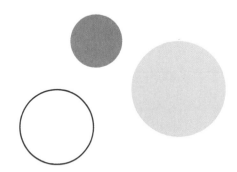

1. In a skillet, heat olive oil and sauté onion, celery, and garlic until onions are translucent. Set aside. In a large mixing bowl, combine beef, pork, milk, breadcrumbs, eggs, onion mixture, salt, chili powder, and pepper. Shape mixture into 1-inch balls. Place meatballs in a single layer on a baking sheet lined with wax paper. Freeze until solid, then transfer to freezer bags until ready to air fry.

2. Place frozen meatballs in a single layer in air fryer basket. Spray with oil. Set temperature to 350 degrees, and air fry for 12 minutes, shaking frequently. Repeat with remaining meatballs.

3. In a Dutch oven, heat barbecue sauce. Add meatballs, and toss to coat thoroughly. Serve warm.

CAPRESE STUFFED PORTABELLAS

Serves 4

2 tablespoons	butter
1 teaspoon	Paula Deen's House Seasoning (see page 40)
4	large portabella mushrooms, stems removed
1	large beefsteak or heirloom tomato, cut into 4 thin slices
1	large fresh mozzarella cheese ball, cut into 4 thin slices
2 ounces	balsamic glaze
4	basil leaves, chopped, for garnish

1. In a small saucepan, melt butter, then stir in House Seasoning. With a paper towel, wipe mushrooms clean; brush with butter mixture. Place one tomato slice in each mushroom, followed by one mozzarella cheese slice.

2. Place 2 mushrooms in air fryer basket. Set temperature to 375 degrees, and air fry for 10 minutes, or until cheese is golden brown. Repeat with remaining mushrooms. In a small saucepan, warm balsamic glaze. Drizzle stuffed portabellas with warm balsamic glaze, sprinkle with chopped basil, and serve warm.

CHEESE-STUFFED MUSHROOMS

Serves 6

24	fresh mushrooms, stems removed
one 10-ounce package	frozen chopped spinach
1 teaspoon	Paula Deen's House Seasoning (see page 40)
½ cup	finely chopped green onions
½ cup	feta cheese, crumbled
2 ounces	cream cheese, room temperature
	oil, for spraying
1 cup	grated Parmesan cheese

1 With damp paper towels, wipe mushroom caps clean. In a colander, thaw spinach and squeeze out as much moisture as possible. In a medium bowl, combine spinach, House Seasoning, green onion, feta cheese, and cream cheese; mix well. Fill mushroom caps with spinach mixture.

2 Working in batches of 10, spray mushrooms with oil and place in air fryer basket. Sprinkle with Parmesan cheese. Set temperature to 375 degrees, and air fry for 6 minutes. Repeat with remaining mushrooms. Serve warm.

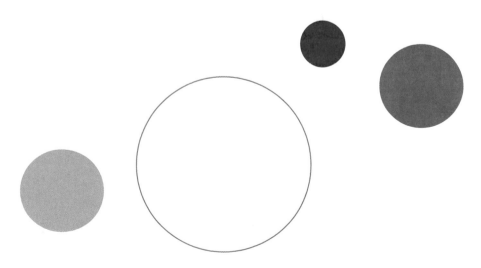

BRIE EN CROÛTE

Serves 4

1 tablespoon	unsalted butter
½ cup	chopped walnuts
⅛ teaspoon	ground cinnamon
one 8-ounce wheel	Brie cheese
¼ cup	brown sugar
1 sheet	frozen puff pastry (from 17.3-ounce package), thawed
	flour, for dusting
1	egg, beaten
	crackers, for serving

1. In a saucepan over medium heat, melt butter. Add walnuts and sauté until golden brown, about 5 minutes. Add cinnamon and stir until walnuts are well coated. Place walnuts on top of Brie, and sprinkle brown sugar on top of nuts.

2. Unfold puff pastry and lay on a lightly floured surface. Place Brie in center of pastry. Gather up edges of pastry, pressing around Brie and gathering at top. Gently squeeze together excess dough and tie with kitchen twine. Brush beaten egg over top and sides of Brie.

3. Set temperature to 400 degrees and preheat air fryer for 5 minutes. Place Brie in air fryer basket lined with parchment paper and air fry for 10 minutes, or until golden brown. Serve warm with crackers.

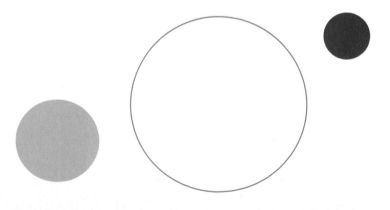

BACON PINWHEELS

Serves 6

¼ cup	cornmeal
1 sheet	frozen puff pastry (from 17.3-ounce package), thawed
1 teaspoon	Dijon mustard
3 ounces	light herb cheese spread
1 cup	crumbled cooked bacon
	oil, for spraying

1. Lightly sprinkle cornmeal on a flat working surface. Unfold pastry dough on top of cornmeal. Spread a thin layer of mustard over dough, leaving a ½-inch border on all sides. Spread cheese over mustard and sprinkle with bacon, leaving border clear. Roll pastry jelly-roll style, and slice into ½-inch-thick pinwheels.

2. Line bottom of air fryer basket with parchment paper. Working in batches, place pinwheels, cut side down, 2 inches apart in a single layer in air fryer basket. Spray with oil. Set temperature to 400 degrees, and air fry for 5 minutes, or until golden brown. Repeat with remaining pinwheels. Serve warm.

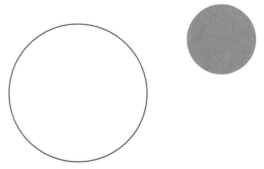

Always a crowd-pleaser, and no one can eat just one.

SCOTCH EGGS

Serves 4

1 pound	bulk pork or turkey sausage
1 tablespoon	all-purpose flour
4	large hard-boiled eggs, peeled, room temperature
½ cup	panko breadcrumbs
½ teaspoon	Paula Deen's House Seasoning (see page 40)
	oil, for spraying

1. Divide sausage into 4 equal portions. Place flour in a shallow dish. Roll each hard-boiled egg in flour, and form a patty around each egg.

2. On a plate, combine breadcrumbs and House Seasoning. Roll each sausage-wrapped egg in bread-crumb mixture, spray with oil, and place in air fryer basket. Set temperature to 400 degrees, and air fry for 10 minutes. Serve warm.

FRIED PIZZA EGG ROLLS

Serves 6

12	egg roll wrappers
¼ teaspoon	Italian seasoning
12 sticks	mozzarella string cheese
36 slices	pepperoni
	oil, for frying
1 cup	pizza sauce

1 Place one egg roll wrapper on a flat surface, corner pointing toward you. Sprinkle with dash of Italian seasoning. Using a pastry brush, lightly brush corners with water. Place 3 pieces pepperoni across center of egg roll wrapper. Place one stick mozzarella cheese along center of pepperoni. Fold bottom corner of wrapper over filling. Fold left and right corners over filling. Tightly roll filled end toward remaining corner, pressing gently to seal. Repeat with remaining egg roll wrappers.

2 Working in batches of 6, spray egg rolls with oil and place in air fryer basket. Set temperature to 400 degrees, and air fry for 10 minutes. Turn and spray with oil halfway through cooking. Repeat with remaining egg rolls. Serve with warm pizza sauce.

GUACAMOLE-STUFFED ONION RINGS

Serves 6

2	avocados, halved, seeded, and peeled
2	Roma tomatoes, seeded and diced
½	medium onion, diced
2 tablespoons	chopped cilantro
	juice of 1 lime
½ teaspoon	kosher salt
¼ teaspoon	cumin
¼ teaspoon	cayenne pepper
¼ teaspoon	black pepper

1	jalapeño pepper, seeded and minced
2	large Vidalia onions, cut into ½-inch slices
1 cup	flour
1 teaspoon	Paula Deen's House Seasoning (see page 40)
2 cups	panko breadcrumbs
2	large eggs
2 tablespoons	milk
	oil, for spraying
	salsa, for dipping

1. To make the guacamole, in a large bowl, mash avocados with fork until chunky. Add tomatoes, onion, cilantro, lime juice, salt, cumin, cayenne pepper, black pepper, and jalapeño pepper. Mix well, cover with plastic wrap, and set aside.

2. On a baking sheet lined with parchment paper, spread onion slices in one layer. Spoon 1 tablespoon of the guacamole in each onion ring and place baking sheet in freezer until stuffed onion rings are solid.

3. In a shallow bowl, combine flour and House Seasoning. Place panko breadcrumbs in another shallow bowl. In a third shallow bowl, beat eggs and stir in milk. Dredge onion rings in flour, gently shaking off excess; dip in egg mixture, shaking off excess; and press into breadcrumb mixture, coating both sides well.

4. Working in batches of 6, spray stuffed onion rings with oil and place in air fryer basket. Set temperature to 400 degrees, and air fry for 12 minutes, or until golden brown. Turn and spray with oil halfway through cooking. Repeat with remaining onion rings. Serve warm with salsa for dipping.

DORITO-CRUSTED FRIED CHEESE

Serves 8

2 pounds	medium Cheddar cheese
1½ cups	flour
4	eggs
1½ cups	Nacho Cheese Doritos
1½ cups	Spicy Nacho Doritos
¼ teaspoon	cayenne pepper
1½ teaspoons	garlic powder
	oil, for spraying

1   Cut cheese into 2-inch squares, then cut squares into triangles. Place flour in a shallow bowl. In another shallow bowl, beat eggs. In a food processor, pulse together both flavors of Doritos until the consistency of breadcrumbs. Place Doritos in a third shallow bowl, and mix in cayenne pepper and garlic powder.

2   Lightly coat cheese triangles with flour; dip in egg, letting excess drip off; and gently roll in Dorito crumbs. Chill coated cheese for at least 1 hour.

3   Working in batches of 6, spray each cheese triangle with oil and place in air fryer basket. Set temperature to 400 degrees, and air fry for 4 minutes. Turn cheese triangles, spray with oil, and air fry for 2 minutes more. Repeat with remaining cheese triangles. Serve warm.

CRISPY RED-PEPPER-JELLY WINGS

Serves 2 to 3

2 tablespoons	olive oil
2 tablespoons	honey
⅛ teaspoon	cayenne pepper
1 tablespoon	baking powder
1 tablespoon	salt
1 pound	chicken wings
	oil, for spraying
2 tablespoons	butter, melted
¼ cup	Paula Deen Red Pepper Jelly

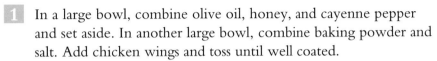

1. In a large bowl, combine olive oil, honey, and cayenne pepper and set aside. In another large bowl, combine baking powder and salt. Add chicken wings and toss until well coated.

2. Place chicken wings in air fryer basket, spray with oil, set temperature to 200 degrees, and air fry for 15 minutes. After five minutes, turn wings, spray with oil, and continue cooking, shaking basket occasionally. Remove wings to reserved honey mixture and toss well to coat. Return wings to air fryer basket, set temperature to 400 degrees, and air fry for 10 minutes, shaking basket occasionally.

3. In a large bowl, combine melted butter and Paula Deen Red Pepper Jelly. Toss wings in jelly mixture and serve warm.

One pound of chicken wings is about 10 to 12 wings, depending on the size of the wings.

BACON-WRAPPED ONION RINGS

Serves 6

½ cup   mayonnaise

2 tablespoons   creamy horseradish

1 tablespoon   ketchup

⅓ teaspoon   cayenne pepper

⅛ teaspoon   dried oregano

¼ teaspoon   salt

1 pinch   black pepper

4 to 5   large Vidalia onions

1 pound   bacon

oil, for spraying

horseradish sauce, for dipping

1   In a small bowl, combine mayonnaise, horseradish, ketchup, cayenne pepper, oregano, salt, and black pepper; set aside.

2   Cut onions into ½-inch-thick slices; remove a few center rings in each slice. Wrap each onion ring with bacon and secure with a toothpick.

3   Working in batches of 4 to 6, place bacon-wrapped onion rings in air fryer basket in a single layer. Set temperature to 400 degrees, and air fry for 10 minutes. Turn and spray with oil once during cooking. Repeat with remaining bacon-wrapped onion rings. Serve warm with horseradish sauce.

CAJUN CHICKEN FRIES
Serves 6

⅓ cup	The Lady & Sons Signature Hot Sauce
½ cup (1 stick)	butter, melted
1 tablespoon	honey
½ teaspoon	salt
½ teaspoon	black pepper
⅓ cup	all-purpose flour
1 pound	skinless boneless chicken breasts, sliced lengthwise into ½-inch-wide strips
	oil, for spraying

1. In a large bowl, whisk together The Lady & Sons Signature Hot Sauce, butter, honey, salt, and pepper.

2. Place flour in a large bowl, and toss chicken strips until coated, shaking off excess flour. Working in batches of 4, spray each chicken strip with oil and place in air fryer basket. Do not overcrowd. Set temperature to 400 degrees, and air fry for 10 minutes. Turn chicken strips, spray with oil, and air fry for 5 minutes more, or until golden brown. Transfer chicken to hot sauce mixture and toss to coat. Repeat with the remaining chicken strips.

3. Serve on a bed of lettuce with white bread.

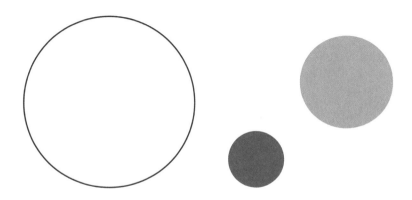

SPICY ONION BLOOM
Serves 2

1	large sweet onion		2	large eggs
1 cup	buttermilk		1 teaspoon	water
1 teaspoon	The Lady & Sons Signature Hot Sauce		1 cup	panko breadcrumbs
				oil, for spraying
1½ cups	all-purpose flour		1 tablespoon	mayonnaise
1 teaspoon	cayenne pepper		1 tablespoon	horseradish
2 tablespoons	Paula Deen's House Seasoning (see page 40)		1 tablespoon	ketchup

1. Cut off top ½ inch of onion and peel. Without slicing through root end of onion, make 12 to 16 cuts toward the center, creating wedge-shaped "petals." Remove about 1 inch of onion from center, and gently separate outer pieces without removing them.

2. In a medium bowl, mix buttermilk and The Lady & Sons Signature Hot Sauce. Completely submerge onion in buttermilk mixture. If onion doesn't fully submerge, add ice water until it does. Refrigerate for 1 hour.

3. In a large bowl, combine flour, cayenne pepper, and House Seasoning. Remove onion from buttermilk mixture and shake off any excess. Place onion in flour mixture, place a plate over top of bowl, and shake onion in flour to distribute flour inside and around outside of onion.

4. In a medium bowl, beat eggs with water. Place breadcrumbs in a shallow dish. Dip flour-coated onion in egg mixture to coat, roll in and sprinkle with breadcrumbs to coat, and spray with oil. Refrigerate for 15 minutes.

5. Spray onion with oil and place in air fryer basket. Set temperature to 400 degrees, and air fry for 5 minutes. Turn onion, spray with oil, and air fry for 3 minutes more.

6. To make dipping sauce, in a small bowl, combine mayonnaise, horseradish, and ketchup. Serve onion warm with dipping sauce on the side.

TURKEY AND CHEESE PINWHEELS

Serves 10

	flour, for dusting
one 12-ounce can	refrigerated crescent dough
¼ pound	thinly sliced turkey breast
8 slices	provolone cheese
2	roasted red peppers
½ teaspoon	dried oregano
	oil, for spraying

1. On a lightly floured surface, spread out crescent dough, pinch interior seams closed, and cut resulting large rectangle in half. On each half of the dough, layer half of the turkey, 4 slices of provolone cheese, and 1 roasted red pepper. Sprinkle with half of the oregano. Roll each square jelly-roll style, and cut each roll into five 1-inch pinwheels.

2. Working in batches of 5, place pinwheels, cut side down, in air fryer basket lined with parchment paper. Do not over-crowd. Spray with oil, set temperature to 350 degrees, and air fry for 5 minutes. Turn pinwheels, spray with oil, and air fry for 3 minutes more. Repeat with remaining pinwheels. Serve warm.

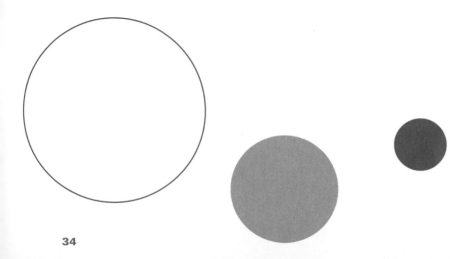

AVOCADO EGG ROLLS

Serves 4

2	large avocados, seeded, peeled, and cut into ½-inch cubes
1 tablespoon	lime juice
½ teaspoon	Paula Deen's House Seasoning (see page 40)
2 tablespoons	minced red onion
⅛ teaspoon	cayenne pepper
8	egg roll wrappers
	oil, for spraying
	salsa or favorite dip, for serving

1. In a medium bowl, combine avocado cubes, lime juice, House Seasoning, onion, and cayenne pepper. Gently mix to retain chunky texture.

2. Place one egg roll wrapper on a flat surface with one corner pointing toward you. Using a pastry brush, lightly brush corners with water. Spoon 2 tablespoons avocado mixture into center of egg roll wrapper. Fold bottom corner of wrapper over filling. Fold left and right corners over filling. Tightly roll filled end toward remaining corner, pressing gently to seal. Repeat with remaining egg roll wrappers.

3. Working in batches of 4, spray each egg roll with oil and place in air fryer basket. Set temperature to 400 degrees, and air fry for 8 minutes. Turn and spray with oil halfway through cooking. Repeat with remaining egg rolls. Serve warm with salsa or your favorite dip.

BACON-WRAPPED
SAUSAGE-STUFFED JALAPEÑOS

Serves 5

½ pound	bulk sausage
8 ounces	cream cheese, softened
10	large jalapeño peppers, halved lengthwise, seeds and membranes removed
10 slices	bacon
	Paula Deen Butt Massage to taste (optional)

1 In a small bowl, combine sausage and cream cheese. Fill each jalapeño pepper half with cream cheese mixture, and press two halves together to form one whole pepper. Wrap each stuffed jalapeño with one bacon slice and secure with toothpicks.

2 Place steam rack in air fryer. Place 4 of the jalapeños on rack, set temperature to 400 degrees, and air fry for 4 minutes. Turn jalapeños and air fry for 4 minutes more. Repeat with remaining jalapeños. Remove toothpicks and sprinkle with Paula Deen Butt Massage, if desired. Serve warm.

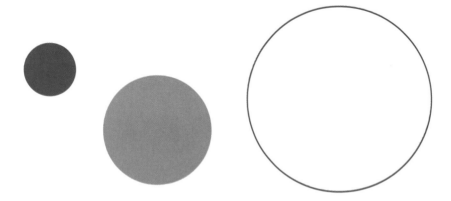

PAULA'S FAVORITES

Southern Fried Chicken • 40

*Roasted Turkey Breast with
Fried Pecan–Bourbon Glaze* • 51

*Buffalo Chicken Livers
with Blue Cheese
Dipping Sauce* • 60

AIR FRYER NAKED HOT CHICKEN WINGS

Serves 4

½ cup (1 stick)	butter
⅓ cup	The Lady & Sons Signature Hot Sauce
2 pounds	chicken wings, each wing cut at joint to yield wingette and drumette
2 tablespoons	peanut oil
1 teaspoon	kosher salt
⅛ teaspoon	cayenne pepper
	oil, for spraying

1 To make buffalo sauce, in a small saucepan over medium heat, combine butter and The Lady & Sons Signature Hot Sauce and heat just until butter melts; keep warm on stovetop. Wash wings, pat dry, and place in a large bowl. Add peanut oil, salt, and cayenne pepper and toss to thoroughly coat wings.

2 Working in batches of 8, place wings in air fryer basket. Set temperature to 400 degrees, and air fry for 25 minutes. Shake occasionally, spraying with oil once during cooking. Repeat with remaining chicken.

3 In a large bowl, toss fried chicken in buffalo sauce, and remove with a slotted spoon to a serving dish.

CRUNCHY COCONUT CHICKEN FINGERS *with* PINEAPPLE SALSA

Serves 4

½ cup	chopped flake sweetened coconut
½ cup	panko breadcrumbs
2 tablespoons	all-purpose flour
1 tablespoon plus 2 teaspoons	brown sugar
1 teaspoon	curry powder
1 pound (about 8)	chicken tenders
½ teaspoon	salt
2	egg whites
	oil, for spraying
two 8-ounce cans	unsweetened pineapple chunks, drained
¼ cup	chopped fresh cilantro
2 teaspoons	lime juice
1	small jalapeño pepper, seeded and minced (optional)

1 On a sheet of wax paper, combine coconut, breadcrumbs, flour, 1 tablespoon of the brown sugar, and curry powder. Sprinkle chicken tenders with salt. In a large bowl, beat egg whites until frothy. Add chicken tenders and toss to coat. One at a time, press chicken tenders into coconut mixture and coat well.

2 Working in batches of 4, spray each chicken tender with oil and place in air fryer basket. Set temperature to 400 degrees, and air fry for 5 minutes. Turn chicken tenders, spray with oil, and air fry for 5 minutes more. Repeat with remaining chicken tenders.

3 To prepare salsa, in a large bowl, toss pineapple, cilantro, lime juice, 2 teaspoons of the brown sugar, and jalapeño pepper, if desired. Serve warm with pineapple salsa on the side.

SOUTHERN FRIED CHICKEN

Serves 4

2½ pounds	chicken, cut into pieces
	Paula Deen's House Seasoning to taste (see below)
3	large eggs
1 cup	The Lady & Sons Signature Hot Sauce
2 cups	self-rising flour
	oil, for spraying

1 Season chicken well with House Seasoning. In a medium bowl, beat together eggs and The Lady & Sons Signature Hot Sauce. Place flour in a shallow dish. Dip chicken pieces in egg mixture, then dredge in flour. Place on a baking sheet lined with parchment paper.

2 Working in batches of 4, spray tops of chicken with oil and place in air fryer basket. Spray chicken again. Set temperature to 350 degrees, and air fry for 15 minutes. Turn chicken, spray with oil, and air fry for 10 minutes more. Turn chicken again, and spray with oil. Increase temperature to 400 degrees, and air fry for 7 minutes. After chicken has reached an internal temperature of 165 degrees, remove to a serving platter and cover to keep warm. Repeat with remaining chicken.

Paula Deen's House Seasoning

1 cup salt
¼ cup freshly ground black pepper
¼ cup garlic powder

In a small bowl, combine salt, pepper, and garlic powder. Store in an airtight container for up to 6 months.

Makes 1½ cups

TURKEY-CRANBERRY MONTE CRISTO

Serves 4

8 slices	potato bread, challah, or other soft bread
1 cup	grated fontina cheese
8 slices	cooked turkey
½ cup	whole cranberry sauce
1 cup	baby arugula leaves
3	eggs
⅓ cup	milk
Pinch	of nutmeg
	butter-flavored oil, for spraying

1 Lay 4 slices of the bread on cutting board. On each slice, place 1 tablespoon of fontina cheese, 2 slices of the turkey, and 2 tablespoons of the cranberry sauce. Equally divide arugula leaves, and layer on top of cranberry sauce. Equally divide remaining fontina, and layer over arugula. Press remaining bread slices firmly onto sandwiches to seal in filling. In a medium bowl, beat eggs, milk, and nutmeg. Dip each sandwich in egg mixture, coating both sides, and then spray each side with oil.

2 Line air fryer basket with parchment paper cut to fit bottom of basket. Working in batches of 2, place sandwiches in air fryer basket. Set temperature to 350 degrees, and air fry for 5 minutes. Turn sandwiches, spray with oil, and air fry for 5 minutes more. Remove to a serving tray and keep warm. Repeat with remaining sandwiches.

SPICY BACON-WRAPPED CHICKEN BITES

Serves 4

5 to 6 slices	bacon
2	skinless boneless chicken breasts, cut into 1-inch cubes
½ cup	brown sugar
¼ teaspoon	salt
¼ teaspoon	cayenne pepper
⅛ teaspoon	black pepper
	oil, for spraying
	barbecue sauce, for dipping

1. Cut each slice of bacon into three pieces. Wrap one piece of bacon around one cube of chicken and fasten with toothpick. In a bowl, combine brown sugar, salt, cayenne pepper, and black pepper. Roll chicken-and-bacon cubes in mixture to coat well.

2. Working in batches of 10, spray each cube with oil and place in air fryer basket in a single layer. Do not overcrowd. Set temperature to 400 degrees, and air fry for 10 minutes. Turn cubes, spray with oil, and air fry for 5 minutes more. Fry longer if bacon should be well done. Repeat with remaining cubes. Serve warm with barbecue sauce on the side.

GLAZED BACON-WRAPPED CHICKEN

Serves 4

⅓ cup	soy sauce
½ cup	orange juice
1 tablespoon	hot sauce
1½ teaspoons	finely chopped garlic
2	skinless boneless chicken thighs, halved
2 slices	bacon, halved crosswise
1 cup	brown sugar
	oil, for spraying

1. In a medium bowl, combine soy sauce, orange juice, hot sauce, and garlic. Add chicken and coat well with marinade. Cover with plastic wrap and refrigerate for 2 hours.

2. Remove chicken from marinade. Wrap one piece of bacon around each piece of thigh. Secure with toothpick. Crumble brown sugar in a small bowl. Dredge each bacon-wrapped thigh in brown sugar to coat evenly.

3. Spray bacon-wrapped chicken with oil and place in air fryer basket. Set temperature to 350 degrees, and air fry for 10 minutes. Turn chicken, spray with oil, and air fry for 15 minutes more, or until bacon is cooked crisp and chicken cooked through.

CHEESIEST FRIED-CHICKEN EMPANADAS *with* CHILI CON QUESO DIP

Serves 6

3 cups	cooked and chopped white-meat chicken (about 5 chicken breasts)
one 8-ounce package	shredded Colby and Monterey Jack cheese blend
4 ounces	cream cheese, softened
1	red bell pepper, chopped
1	jalapeño pepper, seeded and chopped
1 tablespoon	ground cumin
1½ teaspoons	salt
½ teaspoon	freshly ground black pepper
one 15-ounce package	refrigerated pie crust (found in dairy section)
	flour, for dusting
	oil, for spraying

1. In a large bowl, combine chicken, Colby and Monterey Jack cheese blend, cream cheese, red pepper, jalapeño pepper, cumin, salt, and black pepper; set aside.

2. Place one pie crust on a lightly floured surface. Roll into 15-inch circle. Using a 3-inch biscuit cutter, cut into rounds. Combine dough scraps, roll out, and cut more rounds, making total of 12 to 15. Place one dough round on a flat surface. Using a pastry brush, lightly brush edges with water. Place one heaping spoonful of chicken mixture in center of round. Fold dough over filling, pressing edges with a fork to seal. Repeat with remaining rounds and chicken mixture.

Chili con Queso Dip

1 pound Velveeta cheese product

one 16-ounce can diced tomatoes, drained

one 4-ounce can diced green chiles

2 teaspoons The Lady & Sons Signature Hot Sauce

In a saucepan, slowly melt Velveeta cheese over medium-low heat. When cheese is fully melted, add tomatoes, chiles, and The Lady & Sons Signature Hot Sauce, stirring until well combined.

3. Working in batches of 3, spray empanadas on both sides with oil and place in air fryer basket. Set temperature to 350 degrees, and air fry for 7 minutes. Turn empanadas, spray with oil, and air fry for 5 minutes more. Repeat with remaining empanadas. Serve warm topped with *Chili con Queso Dip*, or serve with dip on the side.

You can make empanadas ahead of time and freeze them for up to one month.

BARBECUE CHICKEN PIES

Serves 4

1 teaspoon	butter
½ cup	barbecue sauce
2 cups	shredded deli rotisserie chicken
2	green onions, chopped
one 8-ounce can	refrigerated crescent dinner rolls
½ cup	shredded Cheddar cheese
	oil, for spraying

1. In a medium saucepan, melt butter over medium heat. Stir in barbecue sauce, chicken, and green onions and set aside.
2. Separate dough into 4 rectangles; press together any perforations to seal. Spoon ½ cup chicken mixture on bottom half of each rectangle, and sprinkle with Cheddar cheese. Fold dough over filling and press edges with fork to seal.
3. Working in batches of 2, spray pies with oil on both sides and place in air fryer basket. Set temperature to 350 degrees, and air fry for 12 minutes. Turn and spray with oil halfway through cooking. Repeat with remaining pies. Serve warm.

THE LADY & SONS
CHICKEN FINGERS *with*
HONEY MUSTARD DRESSING
Serves 4

8	chicken tenders (or 2 boneless chicken breasts cut into 4 equal strips)
	Paula Deen's House Seasoning (see page 40) to taste
3 cups	self-rising flour
2 cups	buttermilk
	oil, for spraying

1 Sprinkle chicken tenders with House Seasoning. Place flour in a shallow dish. Place buttermilk in a small bowl. Dredge each chicken tender in flour, dip in buttermilk, and dredge again in flour, shaking off any excess as you work.

2 Working in batches of 4, spray tenders with oil and place in air fryer basket. Do not overcrowd. Set temperature to 400 degrees, and air fry for 5 minutes. Turn tenders, spray with oil, and air fry for 5 minutes more, or until golden brown. Serve warm with *Honey Mustard Dressing* for dipping.

Honey Mustard Dressing

¾ cup mayonnaise
3 tablespoons honey
2 tablespoons yellow mustard
1 tablespoon lemon juice
2 tablespoons orange juice
horseradish to taste

Combine all ingredients except orange juice, and stir well. Add orange juice to thin dressing.

MOLASSES GAME HENS

Serves 2

¼ cup	molasses
2 tablespoons	butter
¼ cup	apple cider vinegar
¼ teaspoon	cayenne pepper, plus more to taste
1½ teaspoons	salt, plus more to taste
2	Cornish hens (1½ pounds each), rinsed and patted dry

1. In a saucepan, combine molasses, butter, vinegar, ¼ teaspoon of the cayenne pepper, and 1½ teaspoons of the salt. Simmer over medium heat for 5 minutes.

2. Lightly sprinkle hens with salt and cayenne pepper, brush each hen with about 2 tablespoons of the molasses mixture, and place in air fryer basket breast side up. Set temperature to 350 degrees, and cook for 35 minutes, or until juices run clear when hens are pierced with a knife in thickest part of thigh. Baste 2 to 3 times with glaze during cooking.

ROASTED TURKEY BREAST *with* FRIED PECAN–BOURBON GLAZE

Serves 6

12 tablespoons (1½ sticks)	butter, softened
½ teaspoon	Paula Deen's House Seasoning (see page 40)
1 tablespoon	chopped fresh parsley
1 tablespoon	minced shallots
1 teaspoon	minced garlic
½	bone-in turkey breast
1 cup	pecan halves
¼ cup	brown sugar
¼ cup	molasses
¼ cup	honey
¼ cup	bourbon

1. In a small bowl, combine 4 tablespoons of the butter, House Seasoning, parsley, shallots, and garlic. Rinse and dry turkey breast with paper towels.

2. Rub turkey breast with butter mixture and place skin side down in air fryer basket lined with parchment paper. Set temperature to 350 degrees, and cook for 20 minutes. Turn turkey breast, increase temperature to 400 degrees, and cook for 15 minutes more, or until internal temperature on a meat thermometer reaches 165 degrees in thickest part of breast. Place turkey breast on a platter, cover, and let rest for 10 minutes before carving.

3. For the glaze, in a skillet over medium heat, melt remaining butter. When butter just begins to bubble, stir in pecan halves. Fry pecan halves gently until light brown. Add sugar, molasses, and honey, and stir until sugar melts. Pour in bourbon and bring to a boil. Lower heat and simmer for 5 minutes until glaze is smooth and syrupy. Let glaze cool slightly, then pour over sliced roasted turkey breast. Serve turkey with extra glaze on the side.

FRIED CHICKEN SALAD

Serves 4

⅓ cup	buttermilk
¼ cup	olive oil
1 teaspoon	fresh lemon juice
½ teaspoon	salt
¾ teaspoon	freshly ground black pepper
3 tablespoons	chopped chives
1 pound	skinless boneless chicken breast
2	large eggs
1 cup	self-rising flour
	oil, for spraying
12 cups	mixed greens
2	plum tomatoes, chopped
½	small Vidalia onion, sliced
	your favorite salad dressing

1. In a small bowl, whisk together buttermilk, olive oil, lemon juice, salt, and ¼ teaspoon of the black pepper. Whisk in chives. Set aside.

2. Cut chicken into 1-inch strips. In a shallow bowl, beat eggs with ¼ cup water. In another shallow bowl, whisk together flour and ½ teaspoon of the black pepper. Dip chicken strips in egg mixture, shaking off any excess. Dredge chicken strips in flour mixture and shake off excess.

3. Working in batches of 6, spray each strip with oil and place in air fryer basket. Set temperature to 400 degrees, and air fry for 20 minutes. Halfway through cooking, turn chicken strips and spray with oil. Repeat with remaining strips.

4. In a large bowl, toss greens, tomatoes, onion, and salad dressing. Divide salad between 4 serving plates, top with fried chicken strips, and drizzle with more salad dressing. Serve immediately.

ASIAN WHOLE ROASTED CHICKEN

Serves 4 to 6

1 tablespoon	brown sugar
3 tablespoons	oyster sauce
1 tablespoon	sesame oil
1 cup	soy sauce
1 tablespoon	cornstarch
¼ teaspoon	black pepper
¼ teaspoon	crushed red pepper flakes
1	whole chicken (3 to 4 pounds), washed and patted dry
	oil, for spraying

For maximum flavor, marinade the chicken a day before you plan to cook it.

1. In a small bowl, combine brown sugar, oyster sauce, sesame oil, soy sauce, cornstarch, black pepper, and red pepper flakes. Pour mixture into large ziplock bag. Add chicken and marinade for 24 hours. Turn occasionally.

2. Pat chicken dry, spray with oil, and place in air fryer basket, breast side down. Set temperature to 350 degrees, and cook for 30 minutes. Turn chicken, spray with oil, and cook for 30 minutes more, or until internal temperature on a meat thermometer reaches 165 degrees in the thickest part of the thigh. Carve and serve warm.

PECAN-CRUSTED CHICKEN TENDERS

Serves 6

2 cups	pecan halves
3 tablespoons	flour
2 tablespoons	Paula Deen's House Seasoning (see page 40)
½ teaspoon	paprika
2	large eggs
1½ pounds	skinless boneless chicken breasts, cut into 1-inch-thick strips
	oil, for spraying

1 In a food processor, pulse ½ cup of the pecans into fine crumbs. In a small bowl, mix processed pecans, flour, House Seasoning, and paprika; set aside. In a food processor, pulse remaining pecans into coarse crumbs and place in another small bowl. In a third small bowl, whisk eggs until beaten. Coat each chicken strip with pecan-and-spice mixture, shaking off any excess; dip in beaten egg, shaking off any excess; and roll in coarsely chopped pecans.

2 Working in batches of 6, spray each chicken tender with oil and place in air fryer basket. Set temperature to 375 degrees, and air fry for 10 minutes, or until golden brown and cooked through. Turn and spray with oil halfway through cooking. Repeat with remaining chicken tenders. Serve warm.

POTATO CHIP–CRUSTED CHICKEN TENDERS

Serves 6

13½ ounces	hickory barbecue potato chips
1 cup	sour cream
1	large egg
½ teaspoon	kosher salt
½ teaspoon	cayenne pepper, optional
2 pounds	skinless boneless chicken breasts, cut into 1-inch-thick strips
	oil, for spraying

1 In a food processor, crush potato chips. Place potato-chip crumbs in a large bowl. In another large bowl, mix sour cream, egg, salt, and cayenne pepper (if desired). Dip chicken strips in sour cream mixture, letting any excess drip off; then roll in crushed chips.

2 Working in batches of 6, spray chicken tenders with oil and place in air fryer basket. Set temperature to 400 degrees, and air fry for 10 minutes, or until golden brown and cooked through. Turn and spray with oil halfway through cooking. Repeat with remaining chicken tenders. Serve warm.

CHICKEN STUFFED WITH PROSCIUTTO AND FONTINA

Serves 2

2	skinless boneless chicken breast halves
4 ounces	fontina cheese, rind removed, cut into 2-inch sticks
2 slices	prosciutto
	salt to taste
	freshly ground black pepper to taste
4 tablespoons	unsalted butter
2 tablespoons	extra-virgin olive oil
1 cup	sliced portabella mushrooms
½ cup	dry white wine
3 sprigs	rosemary
1 bunch	baby arugula
½	lemon, juiced

1. Place chicken breast halves between sheets of wax paper, and using a mallet or rolling pin, pound thin.

2. Wrap each fontina cheese stick with one slice prosciutto and place in center of each flattened chicken breast half. Roll chicken around prosciutto and cheese and secure with toothpicks or butcher's twine. Season chicken rolls with salt and black pepper.

3. In a heavy skillet, heat 2 tablespoons of the butter and 1 tablespoon of the olive oil. Quickly brown chicken rolls over medium heat, 2 to 3 minutes per side. Place chicken rolls in air fryer basket. Set temperature to 350 degrees, and air fry for 7 minutes. Remove chicken rolls to a cutting board and let rest for 5 minutes. Cut rolls at an angle into 6 slices.

4. Reheat skillet, add remaining butter, mushrooms, wine, and rosemary; season with salt and black pepper; and simmer for 10 minutes.

5. In a large bowl, toss arugula leaves in remaining olive oil, lemon juice, salt, and pepper. To serve, arrange chicken and mushrooms on bed of dressed arugula.

BUFFALO CHICKEN LIVERS
with BLUE CHEESE DIPPING SAUCE
Serves 4

1 cup (2 sticks)	butter
½ cup	The Lady & Sons Signature Hot Sauce
1 cup	all-purpose flour
1 teaspoon	salt
½ teaspoon	paprika
½ teaspoon	garlic powder
½ teaspoon	cayenne pepper
½ teaspoon	black pepper
1 pound	chicken livers, soaked in milk
	oil, for spraying
1 cup	blue cheese dressing
4 ounces	blue cheese, crumbled

1. To make buffalo sauce, in a small saucepan, heat butter and The Lady & Sons Signature Hot Sauce until butter is just melted; keep warm until ready to use.

2. In a ziplock or paper bag, combine flour, salt, paprika, garlic powder, cayenne pepper, and black pepper. Place chicken livers in bag and shake gently until coated.

3. Working in batches of 10, spray each chicken liver with oil and place in air fryer basket. Do not overcrowd. Set temperature to 400 degrees, and air fry for 4 minutes. Turn livers, spray with oil, and air fry for 4 minutes more, or until golden brown. Transfer buffalo sauce to a large mixing bowl; in batches, immediately toss fried chicken livers in warm buffalo sauce. Repeat with remaining chicken livers.

4. To make dipping sauce, in a small bowl, stir together blue cheese dressing and crumbled blue cheese.

PAULA'S FAVORITES

Butter Bacon Burgers • 69

*Jamie's Cheeseburgers
in Puff Pastry • 75*

*Fried Pork Chops
with Tomato Gravy • 84*

BARBECUE PORK ROAST

Serves 4 to 6

¼ cup	Worcestershire sauce
¼ cup	soy sauce
2 tablespoons	honey
2 tablespoons	cider vinegar
3 teaspoons	lemon juice
1 teaspoon	mustard
1 teaspoon	salt
½ teaspoon	celery seed
½ teaspoon	black pepper
2 cloves	garlic, minced
1	pork loin roast (3 pounds)
	oil, for spraying
1 cup	Paula Deen barbecue sauce

1. In a small bowl, combine Worcestershire sauce, soy sauce, honey, vinegar, lemon juice, mustard, salt, celery seed, black pepper, and garlic. Place pork loin in a large plastic ziplock bag and pour marinade over pork. Seal and marinade in refrigerator for at least 4 hours (preferably overnight).

2. Remove pork loin from bag, spray with oil, and place in air fryer basket. Discard marinade. Set temperature to 375 degrees, and cook for 45 minutes, or until internal temperature on a meat thermometer reaches 160 to 170 degrees. Remove roast to a platter, cover, and let rest for 10 minutes. Slice and serve with Paula Deen barbecue sauce on the side.

FLANK STEAK BUNDLES
with BALSAMIC GLAZE

Serves 2

1 pound	flank steak, cut into four 3-inch-wide strips
1 tablespoon	Paula Deen's House Seasoning (see page 40)
¼ teaspoon	dried oregano
1 tablespoon	Worcestershire sauce
1	small carrot, cut into matchsticks
½	red bell pepper, cut into matchsticks
4	green onions, cut into matchsticks
	oil, for spraying
½ cup	balsamic glaze

1. Place flank steak strips on cutting board and cover top with plastic wrap. With a meat pounder or rolling pin, gently pound steak to tenderize. Place strips in a shallow baking pan, sprinkle both sides with House Seasoning and oregano, and drizzle with Worcestershire sauce. Marinade for 30 minutes. Make 4 small bundles of equal amounts of carrot, bell pepper, and onion.

2. Pat flank steak strips dry with paper towels. Spray each strip with oil and place one vegetable bundle on bottom of each strip, roll up, and secure each end with toothpicks.

3. Working in batches of 2, spray steak bundles with oil and place in air fryer basket. Set temperature to 375 degrees, and air fry for 5 minutes. Remove bundles to a platter and keep warm. Repeat with remaining bundles.

4. In a saucepan, heat balsamic glaze. Pour over steak, and serve warm.

63

GRILLED APPLE, BACON, AND CHEDDAR SANDWICHES *with* ROASTED RED ONION MAYO

Makes 1 sandwich

two ½-inch-thick slices	sourdough, multigrain, or other hearty bread
4 slices	Cheddar cheese
2 slices	thick-sliced bacon, cooked crisp
½	Granny Smith apple, cored, sliced thin
1 teaspoon	unsalted butter, softened, for spreading

1 Prepare **Roasted Red Onion Mayo**, and spread on both bread slices. Layer one bread slice with 2 Cheddar cheese slices, 2 bacon slices, apple slices, and 2 more Cheddar cheese slices. Top with second mayo–slathered bread slice.

2 Spread both sides of sandwich with unsalted butter, and place in air fryer basket. Set temperature to 350 degrees, and air fry for 5 minutes. Turn sandwich, and air fry for 3 minutes more.

Roasted Red Onion Mayo

1 medium red onion, chopped
2 teaspoons olive oil
salt to taste
freshly ground black pepper to taste
1 cup mayonnaise

In a small bowl, toss red onion, olive oil, salt, and pepper. Place onion mixture in air fryer baking pan and place in air fryer basket. Set temperature to 400 degrees, and air fry for 5 minutes, tossing occasionally, until onions are very soft. Remove onions and let cool. Transfer onions to food processor and pulse until finely chopped. Add mayonnaise to food processor and pulse until smooth and combined.

VEAL LOIN STUFFED WITH ROASTED BELL PEPPERS, GOAT CHEESE, AND BASIL

Serves 6

2	large yellow bell peppers
one 3-ounce package	cream cheese with chives, at room temperature
one 5.3-ounce package	basil-and-roasted-garlic goat cheese (or 6 ounces soft herb goat cheese), at room temperature
1 bunch	arugula, stems trimmed
16	large fresh basil leaves
1	boneless veal loin (3 pounds)
	Paula Deen's House Seasoning (see page 40) to taste
14	oil-packed sun-dried tomatoes, drained
2 tablespoons plus ½ cup (1 stick)	butter, cut into pieces, room temperature
1 tablespoon	olive oil
	salt and pepper to taste
8 slices	bacon
2¾ cups	chicken broth
3	medium shallots, sliced
¼ cup	lemon juice
2 tablespoons	capers
2 tablespoons	chopped fresh parsley

1. Place bell peppers in air fryer basket. Set temperature to 400 degrees, and cook for 5 minutes, or until charred. Place bell peppers in paper bag for 10 minutes to loosen skins, then peel, seed, and stem. Cut bell peppers lengthwise into strips and set aside. In a small bowl, thoroughly blend cream cheese and goat cheese; set aside. Using tongs, plunge arugula and basil in hot water. Remove immediately and place in ice water to blanch. Drain well and set aside.

2 Slice veal open like a book and cover with plastic wrap. With a meat pounder or rolling pin, gently pound veal to an approximately 10 × 12-inch rectangle of even thickness. Season with House Seasoning. Place overlapping arugula leaves down center of veal, forming a 2-inch-wide strip. Cover with half of the bell pepper strips, skinned side up. Arrange sun-dried tomatoes in row on top of bell peppers. Set aside ¼ cup of cheese mixture for sauce, and spoon remaining mixture in an even log over tomatoes. Arrange remaining pepper strips, skinned side up, over cheese. Arrange basil leaves over peppers.

3 Fold one long side of veal over filling and roll veal jelly-roll style. Secure with string and wrap string lengthwise around veal to secure ends. Cover ends of veal with aluminum foil to enclose filling completely. Cover veal in plastic wrap and chill, along with reserved cheese mixture, for at least 6 hours. Veal roast can be prepared 1 day ahead.

4 In a large, heavy skillet, melt 2 tablespoons of the butter with olive oil over medium-high heat. Season veal with salt and pepper and add to skillet. Brown on all sides, turning frequently, about 10 minutes. Place veal roast in air fryer basket. Drape bacon over veal and tuck into ends. Set temperature to 375 degrees, and cook for 35 minutes, or until meat thermometer inserted in thickest part of meat registers 140 degrees. Transfer to work surface and let stand for 10 minutes.

5 In a medium saucepan, boil chicken broth and shallots until mixture is reduced to ½ cup, about 20 minutes. Whisk in lemon juice, capers, and parsley. Reduce heat to low, and gradually whisk in ½ cup of the butter and remaining reserved cheese mixture. Season sauce with salt and pepper.

6 To serve, remove aluminum foil, string, and bacon from veal roast. Cut roast crosswise into even slices. Spoon 2 tablespoons of sauce onto each plate. Top with 2 veal slices.

BUTTER BACON BURGERS

Serves 2

1 pound	lean ground beef
1 stick	butter, cut into small cubes
½ teaspoon	salt
½ teaspoon	freshly ground black pepper
½ teaspoon	garlic powder
2	hamburger buns, split
2 slices	bacon, cooked crisp
	lettuce, for serving
	red onion, sliced, for serving
	tomato, sliced, for serving
	ketchup, for serving
	mayonnaise, for serving

1. In a large bowl, mix together beef, butter, salt, pepper, and garlic powder. Form mixture into 2 patties about 1 inch thick.

2. Spray both patties with oil and place in air fryer basket. Set temperature to 375 degrees, and air fry for 14 minutes, turning once, for medium rare. Remove burgers and keep warm.

3. Place hamburger buns in air fryer basket. Set temperature to 400 degrees, and toast for 3 minutes.

4. Sandwich each burger inside one toasted bun with 1 slice bacon, lettuce, onion, tomato, ketchup, and mayonnaise. Serve warm.

ORANGE BEEF STRIPS
with ORANGE DIPPING SAUCE

Serves 4

1	beef boneless bottom round (1 pound), cut crosswise into 1-inch strips
	salt to taste
	black pepper to taste
1 cup	all-purpose flour
3	large eggs
2 cups	panko breadcrumbs
	oil, for spraying
½ cup	orange marmalade
1 tablespoon	rice wine vinegar
½ teaspoon	Dijon mustard

1 Season beef with salt and pepper. Place flour in a shallow dish. In a shallow bowl, beat eggs. Place breadcrumbs in another shallow dish. One beef strip at a time, dredge in flour, dip in beaten eggs, and then press into breadcrumbs. Place beef strips in a single layer on a baking sheet lined with parchment paper. Spray tops with oil.

2 In a single layer, place beef strips oil side down in air fryer basket and spray tops with oil. Set temperature to 400 degrees, and air fry for 3 minutes. Turn strips, spray with oil, and air fry for 3 minutes more. Remove strips to a platter. Repeat with remaining strips.

3 In a small microwave-safe bowl, stir together marmalade, vinegar, and mustard. Microwave on high for 45 seconds, or until bubbly. Serve beef strips with dipping sauce on the side.

ITALIAN STUFFED PEPPERS

Serves 4

1 teaspoon	olive oil		salt and pepper to taste
½	small onion, diced	4	large bell peppers
2 cloves	garlic, minced		oil, for spraying
½ pound	ground pork	1 tablespoon	Italian seasoning
one 6-ounce can	tomato sauce	1 cup	ricotta cheese
one 6-ounce can	crushed tomatoes	1 cup	shredded mozzarella cheese
1 teaspoon	dried oregano	½ cup	grated Parmesan cheese
¼ teaspoon	crushed red pepper flakes		

1. In a large skillet, heat olive oil over medium heat. Add onion and sauté 2 minutes. Add garlic and sauté 1 minute more, stirring frequently. Add pork and cook until no longer pink. Add tomato sauce, tomatoes, oregano, red pepper flakes, salt, and pepper. Bring to a boil, then reduce heat and simmer until sauce starts to thicken, about 10 to 15 minutes. Remove from heat to cool.

2. Slice peppers in half lengthwise and remove seeds and ribs. Spray inside of peppers with oil and sprinkle with Italian seasoning, salt, and pepper. Layer each pepper with ¼ cup of the meat sauce, 2 tablespoons of the ricotta cheese, followed by 1 to 2 tablespoons more of the meat sauce. Top with 2 tablespoons mozzarella cheese.

3. Working in batches of 2, place stuffed peppers in air fryer basket. Set temperature to 350 degrees, and air fry for 15 minutes, or until cooked through. Top each stuffed pepper with 1 tablespoon of the Parmesan cheese, and air fry for 5 minutes more, or until cheese is golden brown. Repeat with remaining peppers. Serve warm.

SPICY ITALIAN SAUSAGE-STUFFED MUSHROOMS

Serves 6

1 pound	bulk spicy Italian sausage
	oil, for spraying
½ cup	minced red bell pepper
½ cup	minced onion
½ cup	minced celery
3 cloves	garlic, minced
4 tablespoons	half-and-half
½ cup	mozzarella cheese
½ cup	breadcrumbs
¼ teaspoon	salt
¼ teaspoon	freshly ground black pepper
¼ teaspoon	dried oregano
12	jumbo stuffing mushrooms, wiped clean, gills removed
½ cup	grated Parmesan cheese

1 Divide sausage into 1-inch balls. Working in batches, place sausage balls in air fryer basket in a single layer. Do not overcrowd. Spray with oil, set temperature to 400 degrees, and air fry for 4 minutes. Place balls on paper towels to drain. Repeat with remaining sausage.

2 In a small sauté pan sprayed with oil, sauté until tender red bell pepper, onion, celery, and garlic. In a food processor, combine cooked sausage, sautéed vegetables, half-and-half, mozzarella cheese, breadcrumbs, salt, black pepper, and oregano. Pulse until well mixed and somewhat fine.

3 Working in batches of 6, fill each mushroom with generous mound of sausage mixture, spray with oil, sprinkle with Parmesan cheese, and place in air fryer basket. Set temperature to 400 degrees, and air fry for 10 minutes. Repeat with remaining mushrooms. Serve warm.

COUNTRY-FRIED PORK CUTLET
with CREAM GRAVY

Serves 4

1	pork tenderloin (1¼ pounds), sliced on diagonal into four ½-inch-thick pieces	½ cup	all-purpose flour
			kosher salt to taste
1 teaspoon	Paula Deen's House Seasoning (see page 40)		freshly ground black pepper to taste
			oil, for spraying
¾ cup	buttermilk	2 strips	bacon
		¼ cup	water
1 tablespoon	The Lady & Sons Signature Hot Sauce	1 to 1¼ cups	whole milk

1 With a meat mallet, evenly pound pork slices to ¼-inch thickness. Season both sides of pork cutlets with House Seasoning. In a baking dish, whisk buttermilk and The Lady & Sons Signature Hot Sauce. In a separate baking dish, combine flour, salt, and pepper. Dredge pork cutlets in flour, dip in buttermilk mixture, then dredge cutlets in flour again.

2 Working in batches of 2, spray both sides of pork cutlets with oil and place in air fryer basket. Set temperature to 400 degrees, and air fry for 5 minutes. Turn cutlets, spray with oil, and air fry for 5 minutes more. Transfer cutlets to a platter and keep warm. Repeat with remaining cutlets.

3 In a small skillet, heat bacon until fat is rendered. Remove and discard bacon. Add to the skillet flour left over from dredging (you should have about ¼ cup remaining) and whisk until smooth and bubbly, about 1 minute. Add water and 1 cup of the milk to the pan a bit at a time and bring to a boil. Reduce heat to a low simmer and stir until thickened, about 5 minutes. Add milk as necessary to control thickness. Season gravy with salt and lots of black pepper.

4 Plate pork cutlets over grits, and spoon gravy over pork. Serve immediately.

JAMIE'S CHEESEBURGERS IN PUFF PASTRY

Serves 5

1 sheet	frozen puff pastry
1 pound	lean ground beef
½ cup	chopped Vidalia onion, or comparable sweet onion
1 tablespoon	Paula Deen Steak Seasoning Rub
1 tablespoon	steak sauce
5 slices	American, Swiss, or sharp Cheddar cheese
1	egg yolk

1. Let frozen pastry dough sit at room temperature for 20 minutes. Mix beef, onion, Paula Deen Steak Seasoning Rub, and steak sauce with your hands. Form beef mixture into 5 small flat patties.

2. Working in batches of 2, place patties in air fryer basket. Set temperature to 350 degrees, and air fry for 5 minutes per side. Remove patties to a platter and place one slice cheese on each burger.

3. Roll puff pastry sheet to flatten slightly. Cut into 5 even triangles. Cover each beef patty with a piece of puff pastry and wrap it around the bottom, pinching all edges to seal. Whisk together egg yolk and 1 tablespoon of water to make egg wash. Brush each pastry-wrapped patty with egg wash.

4. Line air fryer basket with parchment paper. Working in batches, place cheeseburgers in air fryer basket in a single layer. Set temperature to 400 degrees, and air fry for 5 minutes. Turn cheeseburgers, and air fry for 5 minutes more. Repeat with remaining burgers.

AIR-FRIED NEW YORK STRIP

Serves 2

2	New York strip steaks, 1½ inches thick, room temperature
1 tablespoon	extra-virgin olive oil
1 teaspoon	Paula Deen's House Seasoning (see page 40)

1 Rub steak with oil on both sides, and sprinkle steak on both sides with House Seasoning. Place steaks in air fryer basket, set temperature to 400 degrees, and cook for 6 minutes on each side for medium rare.

2 Serve warm with your favorite topping or steak sauce.

MINI BACON-WRAPPED MEATLOAVES

Serves 4

3 tablespoons	maple syrup
1 teaspoon	Dijon mustard
½ pound	lean ground beef
½ pound	ground pork
1	small onion, minced
2 stalks	celery, minced
½ cup	minced mushrooms
¼ cup	breadcrumbs
2	eggs, beaten
1 tablespoon	tomato paste
¼ cup	tomato sauce
⅛ teaspoon	cayenne pepper
1 teaspoon	Paula Deen's House Seasoning (see page 40)
4 slices	bacon, cut in half

1. In a small bowl, combine maple syrup and mustard. In a large bowl, combine beef, pork, onion, celery, mushrooms, breadcrumbs, beaten egg, tomato paste, tomato sauce, cayenne pepper, and House Seasoning. Form into 4 meatloaves. Wrap each meatloaf with one piece bacon, tucking ends underneath.

2. Working in batches of 2, place in air fryer basket. Brush each meatloaf with maple syrup mixture. Set temperature to 350 degrees, and cook for 15 minutes, turning halfway through cooking. Repeat with remaining 2 loaves. Serve warm.

STUFFED PORK CHOPS *with* GRITS

Serves 2

2	bone-in pork chops, 1½ to 2 inches thick, split to bone
1 pound	bulk sausage
	oil, for spraying
	Paula Deen's House Seasoning (see page 40) to taste
2 cups	water
1¼ cups	milk
1 teaspoon	salt
1 cup	quick-cooking (not instant) grits
½ cup	butter

1 Stuff each pork chop with one-half of the sausage and secure opening with toothpicks or wooden skewers.

2 Spray pork chops liberally with oil, sprinkle both sides with House Seasoning, and place in air fryer basket. Set temperature to 375 degrees, and air fry for 15 minutes, or until internal temperature on a meat thermometer registers 165 to 170 degrees. Turn and spray chops with oil halfway through cooking. Remove toothpicks or skewers from pork chops and keep warm.

3 In a small saucepan, combine water, milk, and salt and bring to a boil. Slowly stir in grits. Stir continuously and thoroughly until grits are well mixed. Return to a boil, cover, lower temperature, and cook for about 30 minutes, stirring occasionally. Add more water if necessary. Grits are done when the consistency of smooth Cream of Wheat. Add butter and stir well.

4 Spoon grits onto plates and top with warm stuffed pork chops.

BEEF EMPANADAS

Yields 24 empanadas

1 cup	mayonnaise	1 tablespoon	garlic salt
1 teaspoon	adobo sauce	2 tablespoons	tomato paste
½	lime, juiced	2 tablespoons	vinegar
3 cups	all-purpose flour	2 teaspoons	ground cumin
1 tablespoon	baking powder	1 teaspoon	chili powder
2 teaspoons	sugar	1 teaspoon	dried oregano
½ teaspoon	salt	1 teaspoon	seasoned salt
½ cup	shortening or lard	5	cloves garlic, minced
1	egg	1	green bell pepper, chopped
¾ cup	chicken stock	1	medium onion, chopped
2 tablespoons	olive oil		oil, for spraying
1 pound	ground beef		

1 For the adobo dip, mix together mayonnaise, adobo sauce, and lime juice. Refrigerate.

2 For the dough, in a large bowl, combine flour, baking powder, sugar, and salt. With a pastry blender or two knives, cut shortening into flour mixture until mixture resembles coarse cornmeal. In a separate bowl, beat egg and whisk in chicken stock. Add egg mixture to flour mixture and knead into dough. Cover and refrigerate for 30 minutes.

3 For the filling, in a large nonstick skillet, heat 1 tablespoon of the olive oil over medium heat. Add beef and garlic salt and heat until beef is cooked through. Drain and set beef aside. In the same pan, heat remaining 1 tablespoon olive oil. Add tomato paste, vinegar, cumin, chili powder, oregano, seasoned salt, garlic, bell pepper, and onion. Cook until vegetables are soft, about 8 to 10 minutes. Add beef, stir, and sauté over low heat for 5 minutes. Mixture should be moist but not wet.

4 Turn dough onto lightly floured work surface and roll out to ¼-inch thickness. Cut into 4- to 6-inch-diameter rounds, depending on your preference. Add meat filling to each round and fold dough in half to enclose filling. Seal by pressing edges with tines of a fork. You can refrigerate uncooked empanadas for up to 3 hours.

5 Working in batches of 4, spray empanadas on both sides with oil and place in air fryer basket. Set temperature to 350 degrees, and air fry for 5 minutes. Turn empanadas, spray with oil, and air fry for 5 minutes more. Remove empanadas to a serving platter. Serve warm with adobo dip.

You may skip the dough preparation and purchase frozen empanada wrappers.

FRENCH ONION PORK CHOPS

Serves 4

2	eggs
one 19-ounce box	French onion soup mix (2 packets)
½ cup	breadcrumbs
4	boneless pork chops (4 ounces each)
	oil, for spraying

1 In a shallow dish, beat eggs. In another shallow dish, combine French onion soup mix and breadcrumbs. Coat each pork chop with egg, and press both sides into breadcrumb mixture.

2 Working in batches of 2, spray both sides of pork chops with oil and place in air fryer basket. Set temperature to 375 degrees, and air fry for 15 minutes. Turn chops and spray with oil halfway through cooking. Serve warm.

AIR-FRIED AVOCADO
with EGGS AND BACON

Serves 2

1	ripe avocado
2	eggs
2 slices	bacon, cooked and crumbled
	oil, for spraying
1 teaspoon	chopped cilantro or parsley

1. Cut avocado in half and remove seed. Scoop out just enough flesh to fit one egg without spilling. Drop one egg into each avocado half and sprinkle with crumbled bacon.

2. Place avocado halves in air fryer basket and spray with oil. Set temperature to 350 degrees, and cook for 5 minutes, or until whites are set and yolks are runny. Sprinkle with cilantro or parsley and serve warm.

FRIED PORK CHOPS
with TOMATO GRAVY
Serves 2

2	bone-in center-cut pork chops (½ pound each), 1 inch thick
½ teaspoon	salt, plus more for seasoning pork
¼ teaspoon	black pepper, plus more for seasoning pork
¼ teaspoon	garlic powder
	oil, for spraying
4 tablespoons (½ stick)	unsalted butter
2 tablespoons	finely chopped onion
¼ cup	all-purpose flour
1½ cups	whole milk
1½ cups	chicken broth or water
one 14½-ounce can	tomatoes, drained

1. Lightly sprinkle pork chops on both sides with salt, pepper, and garlic powder. Spray each pork chop on both sides with oil and place in air fryer basket. Set temperature to 400 degrees, and air fry for 10 minutes. Turn chops, spray with oil, and air fry for 10 minutes more.

2. While pork chops are cooking, melt butter in a small skillet. Add onion and sauté, stirring, until softened, about 5 minutes. Reduce heat if onion browns too quickly. Sprinkle flour over onion and cook, stirring, for 1 minute more. Slowly whisk in milk and then broth. Simmer until thickened, about 5 minutes. Whisk in tomatoes, ½ teaspoon of the salt, and ¼ teaspoon of the pepper. Spoon tomato gravy over pork chops and serve.

PAULA'S FAVORITES

Air-Fried Shrimp · 93

Maple-Glazed Salmon with Pineapple Salsa · 96

Stuffed Bacon-Wrapped Shrimp · 98

CRAWFISH ROLLS

Serves 4

2 cloves	garlic, minced
1	red bell pepper, chopped
1	shallot, diced
2 tablespoons	butter
2 pounds	crawfish tails
1 tablespoon	Cajun seasoning
2 cups	raw spinach
1½ cups	shredded white Cheddar cheese
1 cup	sweet corn
1 cup	black beans
1 cup	cornstarch
1	egg
8	spring roll wrappers
	oil, for spraying

1. In a large sauté pan over medium heat, sauté garlic, bell pepper, and shallot in butter. Add crawfish tails and Cajun seasoning and stir until blended. Cook until tails turn pink and become opaque. Remove from heat and place in a bowl to cool. After crawfish mixture cools, add spinach, white Cheddar cheese, corn, and black beans.

2. Place cornstarch in a shallow dish. In another shallow dish, beat egg. Place 2 ounces of crawfish mixture in middle of each spring roll wrapper, wash edges with beaten egg, and seal. Dredge rolls in cornstarch.

3. Working in batches of 4, spray each egg roll with oil and place in air fryer basket in a single layer. Do not overcrowd. Set temperature to 400 degrees, and air fry for 4 minutes. Turn rolls, spray with oil, and air fry for 4 minutes more, or until golden brown. Serve warm.

CRISPY TORTILLA-CRUSTED TILAPIA

Serves 2

½ cup	crushed tortilla chips
2 tablespoons	butter, melted
1 teaspoon	finely grated lime zest
¼ teaspoon	dried basil
2	skinless tilapia fillets (4 ounces each)
½ teaspoon	Paula Deen's House Seasoning (see page 40)

1 In a medium bowl, combine crushed tortilla chips, melted butter, lime zest, and basil.

2 Place tilapia fillets in air fryer basket lined with parchment paper. Season with House Seasoning and press tortilla mixture firmly into tops of fish. Set temperature to 400 degrees, and air fry for 6 minutes, or until fish is opaque and just cooked through and tortilla crumbs are golden around the edges.

PEEL AND EAT SHRIMP

Serves 4

2 pounds	shrimp, shells on
3 tablespoons	crab boil seasoning
1	lemon, cut into wedges, for serving
	cocktail sauce, for serving

1. Pour 1 cup water in bottom of air fryer pan. Set temperature to 400 degrees, and heat for 10 minutes.

2. Place shrimp in air fryer basket, sprinkle with crab boil, and toss to coat. Set temperature to 375 degrees, and air fry for 7 minutes, shaking occasionally, or until shrimp are pink. Chill and serve with lemon wedges and cocktail sauce.

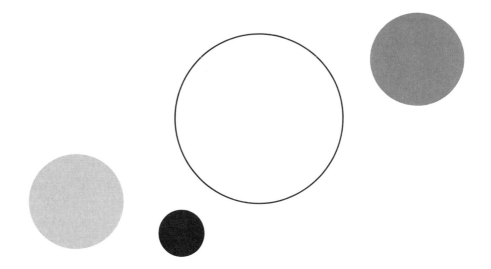

TUNA MELT

Serves 2

one 6-ounce can	white tuna packed in water, drained
⅓ cup	mayonnaise (or salad dressing)
1 tablespoon	minced celery
1 tablespoon	minced Vidalia onion
1 teaspoon	minced parsley
¼ teaspoon	Paula Deen's House Seasoning (see page 40)
2 slices	whole grain, sourdough, or rye bread, toasted
4 slices	Cheddar cheese
2 slices	tomato

1 In a medium bowl, break up tuna with a fork. Add mayonnaise, celery, onion, parsley, and House Seasoning; mix well.

2 Top one toast slice with tuna mixture and 2 slices Cheddar cheese and place in air fryer basket. Set temperature to 400 degrees, and air fry for 2 minutes. Top with 1 slice tomato and air fry for 2 minutes more. Repeat with remaining ingredients and serve warm.

SHAM BAM SHRIMP

Serves 4

½ cup	mayonnaise
1 tablespoon	Thai sweet chili sauce
1½ tablespoons	Sriracha hot pepper sauce
¼ teaspoon	salt
¼ teaspoon	black pepper
1 pound	shrimp, peeled and deveined
½ cup	cornstarch
	oil, for spraying
1 head	lettuce, shredded, for serving
1	spring onion, sliced

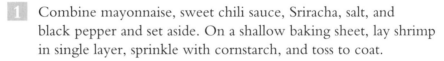

1. Combine mayonnaise, sweet chili sauce, Sriracha, salt, and black pepper and set aside. On a shallow baking sheet, lay shrimp in single layer, sprinkle with cornstarch, and toss to coat.

2. Working in batches of 10, spray each shrimp with oil and place in air fryer basket. Do not overcrowd. Set temperature to 400 degrees, and air fry for 3 minutes. Turn shrimp, spray with oil, and air fry for 3 minutes more. Repeat with remaining shrimp.

3. Toss warm fried shrimp in mayonnaise mixture and serve on a bed of lettuce topped with spring onion.

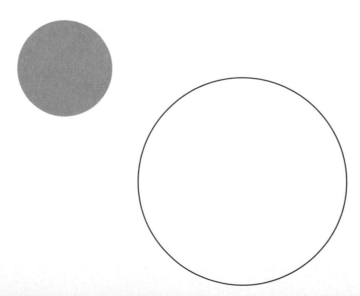

CRAB CAKES
Serves 4

1 tablespoon	mayonnaise
1 teaspoon	spicy mustard
1 teaspoon	ketchup
24	buttery crackers
2 tablespoons	butter
1	celery stalk, minced
1	small onion, minced
1	small red bell pepper, minced
½ teaspoon	crab seasoning
8 ounces	lump crab meat
1 teaspoon	lemon juice
1 teaspoon	cayenne pepper sauce
1 teaspoon	Worcestershire sauce
1	large egg, beaten
1 cup	panko breadcrumbs
	oil, for spraying

1 For the sauce, in a small bowl, blend mayonnaise, mustard, and ketchup and set aside.

2 In the bowl of a food processor fitted with a metal blade, pulse crackers until finely crumbled. In a small skillet, melt butter. Add celery, onion, and red pepper and sauté until tender. In a large bowl, combine crumbled crackers, crab seasoning, crab meat, sautéed vegetables, lemon juice, cayenne pepper sauce, Worcestershire sauce, and beaten egg. Mix gently by hand.

3 Place breadcrumbs in a shallow glass baking dish. Form a patty with ¼ cup of the crab mixture and press into breadcrumbs, covering both sides. Repeat with remaining crab mixture.

4 Working in batches of 3, spray crab cakes with oil and place in air fryer basket. Set temperature to 400 degrees, and air fry for 7 minutes. Serve warm with sauce on the side.

AIR-FRIED SHRIMP

Serves 4

1 cup	milk
1 cup	buttermilk
1 cup	The Lady & Sons Signature Hot Sauce
2 cups	self-rising flour
¼ cup	self-rising cornmeal
3 tablespoons	salt
2 tablespoons	black pepper
2 pounds	medium shrimp, peeled and deveined, tails intact
	oil, for spraying

1. In a shallow dish, whisk together milk, buttermilk, and The Lady & Sons Signature Hot Sauce. In another shallow dish, whisk together flour, cornmeal, salt, and pepper. Pat shrimp dry with paper towels. Dredge each shrimp in flour mixture, then dip in milk mixture, and then dredge in flour mixture again.

2. Working in batches of 10, spray shrimp on all sides with oil and place in air fryer basket in a single layer. Set temperature to 400 degrees, and air fry for 5 minutes. Turn shrimp, spray with oil, and air fry for 5 minutes more. Repeat with remaining shrimp.

SALMON BURGERS
with SUN-DRIED TOMATO MAYONNAISE

Serves 4

¼ cup	mayonnaise (regular or light)
1 tablespoon	coarsely chopped oil-packed sun-dried tomatoes
1 teaspoon	lemon juice
2 dashes	The Lady & Sons Signature Hot Sauce
1½ pounds	skinless salmon fillets, finely chopped
¼ cup	panko breadcrumbs (whole-wheat or regular)
1 tablespoon	sweet pickle relish
1 tablespoon	Dijon mustard
¾ teaspoon	salt
½ teaspoon	freshly ground pepper
4	hamburger buns, split
4	lettuce leaves, for serving
4	tomato slices, for serving

1 In a blender or food processor, puree mayonnaise, sun-dried tomatoes, lemon juice, and The Lady & Sons Signature Hot Sauce until nearly smooth (flecks of tomato will remain). Place in a small bowl and refrigerate until ready to use.

2 In a medium bowl, combine salmon, breadcrumbs, relish, mustard, salt, and pepper. Mix gently and shape into 4 patties.

3 Working in batches of 2, spray patties with oil on both sides and place in air fryer basket. Set temperature to 350 degrees, and air fry for 5 minutes. Turn patties, spray with oil, and air fry for 5 minutes more.

4 Spread sun-dried tomato mayonnaise on bottom half of each hamburger bun. Top with salmon burger, lettuce, tomato, and other bun half. Serve warm.

MAPLE-GLAZED SALMON
with PINEAPPLE SALSA

Serves 2

2	salmon fillets (6 ounces each), skin on
1 tablespoon	maple syrup
1 tablespoon	teriyaki sauce
1 tablespoon	pineapple juice
1 teaspoon	minced fresh ginger
1 clove	garlic, mashed
	oil, for spraying

1. Score salmon fillet skin and place fillets in a ziplock plastic bag. In a nonreactive bowl or measuring cup, combine maple syrup, teriyaki sauce, pineapple juice, ginger, and garlic. Pour marinade over fillets and refrigerate for at least 1 hour (preferably overnight).

2. Place fillets skin side up in air fryer basket lined with parchment paper and spray with oil. Set temperature to 400 degrees, and air fry for 5 minutes, or to desired doneness. Served with *Pineapple Salsa* on the side.

Pineapple Salsa

1 medium ripe tomato, chopped into small cubes

¼ cup chopped red bell pepper

2 pickled jalapeño slices, deseeded and finely chopped

½ cup pineapple chunks, fresh or canned

1 teaspoon salt

1 tablespoon sugar

In a small nonreactive saucepan, combine tomato, bell pepper, jalapeño, pineapple, salt, and sugar. Simmer over low heat for 5 minutes. Let cool. Refrigerate until ready to serve.

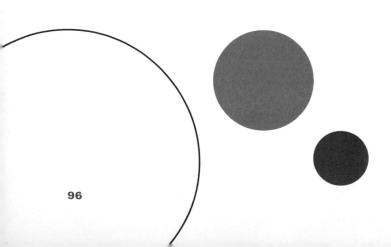

STUFFED BACON-WRAPPED SHRIMP

Serves 4

1	jalapeño pepper, seeded and julienned
8	extra-large shrimp, butterflied with tails on
4 ounces	shredded mozzarella cheese
4 slices	bacon, cut in half
	oil, for spraying

1. Place a sliver of jalapeño pepper in each shrimp, followed by ½ ounce of the mozzarella cheese. Close each shrimp around filling, wrap with bacon, and secure with a toothpick.

2. Working in batches of 4, spray wrapped shrimp with oil and place in air fryer basket. Set temperature to 375 degrees, and air fry for 8 minutes. Turn shrimp and spray with oil halfway through cooking. Repeat with remaining wrapped shrimp. Serve warm.

SALMON CROQUETTES

Serves 4

one 14.75-ounce can	salmon, drained
1	large egg, beaten
2 tablespoons	sliced green onion
½ cup	breadcrumbs
	oil, for spraying

1 In a medium bowl, combine salmon, egg, green onion, and ¼ cup of the breadcrumbs. Form mixture into patties and dust with additional breadcrumbs.

2 Spray 2 patties with oil on both sides and place in air fryer basket. Set temperature to 400 degrees, and air fry for 5 minutes. Turn patties, spray with oil, and air fry for 5 minutes more. Repeat with remaining patties. Serve warm.

EASY FISH TACOS

Serves 8

½ cup	mayonnaise
2 teaspoons	adobo sauce, from canned chipotle peppers
4	tilapia fillets (5 ounces each)
1 tablespoon	Paula Deen's House Seasoning (see page 40)
	oil, for spraying
8	corn tortillas
¼ head	Savoy cabbage, shredded
	salt and pepper to taste

1 In a small bowl, whisk together mayonnaise and adobo sauce. Set aside.

2 Working in batches of 2, season tilapia fillets on both sides with House Seasoning, spray fillets on both sides with oil, and place in air fryer basket. Set temperature to 350 degrees, and air fry for 6 minutes. Turn fillets and spray with oil halfway through cooking. Remove fillets to a plate and flake into chunky pieces with a fork. Repeat with remaining tilapia fillets.

3 Spread mayonnaise mixture on tortillas and top with fish and cabbage. Season with salt and pepper before serving.

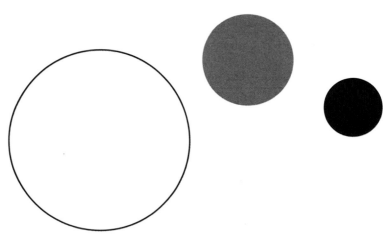

COCONUT-FRIED SHRIMP
with DIPPING SAUCE

Serves 4 to 6

½ teaspoon	crushed red pepper flakes
4 teaspoons	rice wine vinegar
½ cup	orange marmalade
½ cup	all-purpose flour
1 teaspoon	salt
½ teaspoon	baking powder
⅔ cup	water
2 cups	shredded sweetened coconut
½ cup	breadcrumbs
1 pound	medium or large shrimp, peeled and deveined
	oil, for spraying

1 For the dipping sauce, in a medium saucepan, combine red pepper flakes, vinegar, and marmalade and simmer on low heat for 10 minutes, stirring occasionally.

2 In a large bowl, whisk together flour, salt, and baking powder. Add water and whisk until smooth. Let batter stand for 15 minutes. In a shallow bowl, toss together coconut and breadcrumbs. Place shrimp in batter and coat well. Remove shrimp, one at a time, and press into coconut mixture. Coat well.

3 Spray shrimp on all sides with oil and place in air fryer basket in a single layer. Set temperature to 400 degrees, and air fry for 5 minutes. Turn shrimp, spray with oil, and air fry for 5 minutes more. Repeat with remaining shrimp. Serve warm with dipping sauce on the side.

SOUTHERN FRIED OYSTERS
with SPICY DIPPING SAUCE
Serves 4

⅓ cup	Paula Deen Vidalia Onion Peach Marinade
1 tablespoon	sour cream
½ cup	all-purpose flour
2	large eggs
3 tablespoons	The Lady & Sons Signature Hot Sauce
1 cup	panko breadcrumbs
12	plump oysters, freshly shucked
	oil, for spraying
	kosher salt to taste

1 For the sauce, in a small bowl, combine Paula Deen Vidalia Onion Peach Marinade and sour cream; mix well and set aside.

2 Place flour in a small bowl. In a second bowl, whisk together eggs and The Lady & Sons Signature Hot Sauce. In a third bowl, crush breadcrumbs a little finer. Dredge oysters in flour, shaking off any excess. Dip oysters in egg mixture, shaking off any excess. Roll oysters in breadcrumbs and place in a single layer on baking sheet lined with parchment paper. Spray with oil and refrigerate for 30 minutes.

3 Working in batches of 6, place oysters in air fryer basket in a single layer and spray with oil. Set temperature to 400 degrees, and air fry for 4 minutes. Turn oysters, spray with oil, and air fry for 4 minutes more. Remove from basket and immediately sprinkle with salt. Repeat with remaining oysters. Serve warm with spicy dipping sauce.

SALT AND
VINEGAR CHIP–FRIED COD
Serves 2

¼ cup	buttermilk
½ teaspoon	Paula Deen's House Seasoning (see page 40)
2	cod fillets (6 ounces each)
3 cups	salt and vinegar kettle-cooked potato chips
	oil, for spraying

1 In a medium bowl, mix buttermilk and House Seasoning. Add cod fillets and marinade for 5 minutes. In a food processor, pulse potato chips until well crushed. Place crushed potato chips in a shallow dish. One at a time, remove cod fillets from buttermilk mixture and press firmly into crushed chips, covering entire fillet.

2 Spray each cod fillet with oil on both sides and place in air fryer basket. Set temperature to 400 degrees, and air fry for 12 minutes. Turn and spray with oil halfway through cooking. Serve warm.

AIR-FRIED SOFT-SHELL CRABS

Serves 2

1	large egg
1 teaspoon	The Lady & Sons Signature Hot Sauce
½ cup	cornmeal
½ cup	self-rising flour
¼ teaspoon	salt
¼ teaspoon	freshly ground black pepper
4	soft-shell crabs
	oil, for spraying

1 In a medium bowl, beat egg and whisk in hot sauce. In another bowl, mix cornmeal, flour, salt, and black pepper. Dip crabs in egg mixture, then dip in flour mixture, shaking off excess.

2 Spray crabs well with oil and place in air fryer basket. Set temperature to 400 degrees, and air fry for 5 minutes. Turn crabs, spray with oil, and air fry for 5 minutes more. Serve warm.

FRIED CATFISH

Serves 4

4	catfish fillets
	salt to taste
	black pepper to taste
1 cup	buttermilk
2 tablespoons	hot sauce
1 cup	self-rising flour
1 cup	yellow cornmeal
1 teaspoon	crab boil seasoning
1 teaspoon	garlic powder
	oil, for spraying

1 Season catfish fillets on both sides with salt and pepper. In an 8 × 8–inch casserole dish, mix buttermilk and hot sauce. Add catfish fillets, completely covering with liquid. In a shallow dish, whisk together flour, cornmeal, crab boil seasoning, and garlic powder.

2 Remove catfish fillets from buttermilk mixture, letting excess drip off. Dredge catfish fillets on both sides in cornmeal mixture, gently pressing down to coat well. Place coated fillets on baking sheet lined with parchment paper and spray with oil on both sides. Sprinkle with cornmeal mixture and refrigerate for 30 minutes.

3 Place 2 catfish fillets in air fryer basket and spray well with oil. Set temperature to 400 degrees, and air fry for 10 minutes. Gently turn fillets, spray with oil, and air fry for 5 minutes more, or until golden brown and cooked through. Repeat with remaining fillets. Serve warm.

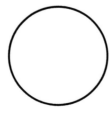

BAKED LOBSTER TAIL

Serves 2

2	lobster tails (6 ounces each)
3 tablespoons	clarified butter
3 tablespoons	fresh lemon juice
⅛ teaspoon	paprika
½ teaspoon	Paula Deen's House Seasoning (see page 40)

1 To butterfly each lobster tail, cup lobster tail in one hand with hard top shell up. Using kitchen shears, cut through top of shell and meat to the tail. Using thumbs and fingers, spread apart cut shell and loosen from meat. Separate meat down center cut, keeping attached near tail.

2 In a small bowl, combine butter, lemon juice, paprika, and House Seasoning. Place lobster tails on 2 separate sheets of aluminum foil and drizzle with butter mixture. Fold up ends to completely seal. Place lobsters in air fryer basket, set temperature to 375 degrees, and cook for 12 minutes. Serve warm.

LOW COUNTRY BOIL

Serves 2

1 cup	dry white wine (or water)
2 ears	corn, cut in half
½ pound	medium shrimp, shells on
6	littleneck clams
1 pound	andouille sausage, cut into 1-inch pieces
2	lobster tails (4 ounces each)
1	lemon, cut in half
1 tablespoon	shrimp boil seasoning

1 Place wine in bottom pan of air fryer, set temperature to 400 degrees, and preheat for 5 minutes.

2 Add air fryer basket to air fryer pan, leaving wine in place, and fill basket with corn, shrimp, clams, andouille sausage, and lobster tails. Squeeze lemon halves over top of seafood mixture, sprinkle with shrimp boil seasoning, and place lemon halves on top of lobster tails. Set temperature to 350 degrees, and steam for 10 minutes. Serve warm.

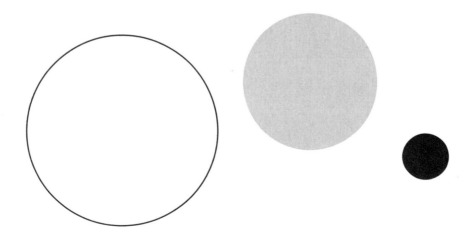

SESAME SEED–CRUSTED TUNA STEAKS

Serves 2

2 tablespoons	soy sauce
3 tablespoons	bourbon
¾ teaspoon	black pepper
4 tablespoons	olive oil
4 tablespoons	sesame oil
2	tuna steaks (8 ounces each)
2 tablespoons	honey
1	lime, juiced
1 cup	sesame seeds
	oil, for spraying
2 cups	arugula
4	radishes, trimmed and sliced
½ cup	sliced red onion
½ cup	sliced red bell pepper

1   In a large bowl, whisk together soy sauce, bourbon, black pepper, 2 tablespoons of the olive oil, and 2 tablespoons of the sesame oil. Add tuna steaks and flip to coat both sides. Cover tightly with plastic wrap and marinate for 1 hour in refrigerator.

2   To make a honey dressing, in a small bowl, combine remaining olive oil, remaining sesame oil, honey, and lime juice; mix well.

3   Place sesame seeds in a shallow dish. Press both sides of marinated tuna steaks into sesame seeds, spray with oil, and place in air fryer basket. Set temperature to 400 degrees, and air fry for 6 minutes. Turn and spray tuna steaks with oil halfway through cooking.

4   Cut tuna steaks diagonally into ½-inch-thick slices. Divide arugula, radishes, red onion, and bell peppers between 2 salad plates, and place sliced tuna on top. Drizzle with honey dressing and serve.

CRAB BALLS *with* TARTAR SAUCE

Yields 2 dozen

3 slices	bread, crust removed, processed into breadcrumbs
⅓ cup	heavy cream
1 pound	lump crab meat, picked free of shell
1	egg, beaten
1 tablespoon plus 1 cup	mayonnaise
1 tablespoon	Worcestershire sauce
1 teaspoon	Paula Deen Silly Salt
1 teaspoon	Paula Deen's House Seasoning (see page 40), and more to taste
1 tablespoon	finely chopped fresh parsley
	oil, for spraying
1	white onion, cut into fourths
½ cup	dill chips
	fresh lemon juice to taste
	freshly ground pepper to taste

1 In a large bowl, moisten breadcrumbs with heavy cream. Mix in crab, beaten egg, 1 tablespoon of the mayonnaise, Worcestershire sauce, Paula Deen Silly Salt, House Seasoning, and parsley. Shape crab mixture into walnut-size balls.

2 Working in batches of 10, spray crab balls with oil and place in air fryer basket. Set temperature to 400 degrees, and air fry for 5 minutes. Turn crab balls, spray with oil, and air fry for 2 minutes more. Repeat with remaining crab balls.

3 To make tartar sauce, in a food processor, pulse 1 cup of the mayonnaise, onion, dill chips, lemon juice, pinch of House Seasoning, and pepper to desired chunkiness.

4 Serve crab balls hot with tartar sauce on the side. Crab balls can be made ahead of time and reheated before serving.

PAULA'S FAVORITES

*Roasted Brussels Sprouts
with Lemon Zest · 121*

EGG CRISPS

Serves 2

2 slices	white bread, crusts removed
1 tablespoon	butter, room temperature
2	large eggs
	salt and freshly ground pepper to taste
½ tablespoon	grated Parmesan cheese
2 slices	bacon, cooked and crumbled

1 Spread one side of each slice of bread with butter. Press slices, butter side up, into 2- to 4-ounce ramekins. Place ramekins in air fryer basket. Set temperature to 350 degrees, and air fry for 5 minutes, or until pale golden.

2 Crack one egg into each ramekin. Season with salt and pepper. Sprinkle each egg with half of the Parmesan cheese. Air fry for 5 minutes, or until whites are set but yolks are still nice and runny. Serve topped with crumbled bacon.

Crumble up these crisps and use as a salad topping.

TOMATO TARTS

Serves 4

1 sheet	frozen puff pastry
	all-purpose flour, for dusting
	oil, for spraying
½ cup	grated white Cheddar cheese
2	plum tomatoes, cut into ¼-inch slices
	salt to taste
	freshly ground black pepper to taste
2 tablespoons	finely chopped thyme
½ cup	freshly grated Parmesan cheese

1 Remove puff pastry from freezer and allow to thaw for 20 minutes. Unfold pastry dough on a lightly floured surface. Spray dough with oil, and using a 1½- or 2-inch-diameter biscuit cutter, cut out 4 rounds of dough.

2 Spray bottom of air fryer basket with oil, place all pastry rounds in basket, and poke holes in surface of pastry with a fork. Top each pastry round with one-quarter of the Cheddar cheese and one tomato slice. Sprinkle each with salt, pepper, thyme, and one-quarter of the Parmesan cheese. Set temperature to 400 degrees, and air fry for 6 minutes. Let cool for 3 minutes before serving.

FRIED ARTICHOKES

Serves 4

1	lemon, juiced
2	medium artichokes, trimmed and quartered, choke removed
2	eggs
1 cup	Parmesan cheese Italian breadcrumbs
1 teaspoon	Paula Deen's House Seasoning (see page 40)
	oil, for spraying

1. In a bowl with enough water to cover artichokes, add lemon juice and artichokes, and let sit for 15 minutes. Drain artichokes and discard liquid. In a medium saucepan, bring water to a boil, and blanch artichoke quarters for 10 minutes. Drain artichokes and set aside.

2. In a shallow bowl, beat eggs. In a shallow dish, mix breadcrumbs and House Seasoning. Dip each artichoke quarter in beaten egg, then gently roll in breadcrumb mixture.

3. Spray artichoke quarters with oil and place in air fryer basket. Set temperature to 400 degrees, and air fry for 10 minutes, shaking 3 times during cooking. Serve warm.

AIR-FRIED AVOCADO

Serves 4

2	ripe-but-firm avocados, peeled and pitted, each cut into 8 slices
2 tablespoons	lime juice
1 cup	panko breadcrumbs
½ teaspoon	salt
⅛ teaspoon	cayenne pepper
	oil, for spraying
	salsa, for serving
	sour cream, for serving

SIDES

1. Place avocado slices in a single layer on a baking sheet lined with parchment paper and sprinkle with lime juice. In a shallow bowl, crush breadcrumbs a little finer, then add salt and cayenne pepper and mix well. Carefully coat each avocado slice in breadcrumb mixture and return to baking sheet.

2. Working in batches of 8, spray each avocado slice on both sides with oil and place in air fryer basket in a single layer. Set temperature to 400 degrees, and air fry for 6 minutes. Shake occasionally, and spray with oil halfway through. Remove avocados to a serving dish and keep warm. Repeat with remaining avocados. Serve warm with salsa and sour cream on the side.

ROASTED BRUSSELS SPROUTS
with LEMON ZEST

Serves 4

1 pound	Brussels sprouts, trimmed and cut in half lengthwise
3 tablespoons	olive oil
1 teaspoon	salt
½ teaspoon	freshly ground black pepper
2 tablespoons	lemon zest

1 In a small bowl, combine Brussels sprouts, olive oil, salt, and black pepper; toss to coat evenly.

2 Place Brussels sprouts in air fryer basket. Do not overcrowd. Set temperature to 375, and cook for 15 minutes, shaking occasionally. Sprinkle with lemon zest and serve warm.

SIDES

121

AIR-FRIED
GLUTEN-FREE GREEN BEANS

Serves 6

1	large egg
1 cup	buttermilk
1 cup	gluten-free coating
1 teaspoon	Cajun seasoning
1 pound	green beans, stems trimmed
	oil, for spraying

1. In a medium bowl, beat egg, then add buttermilk and stir. In a shallow dish, combine gluten-free coating and Cajun seasoning. Dip green beans in buttermilk mixture, then roll in coating mixture. Place in a single layer on a baking sheet lined with parchment paper.

2. Working in batches of 16, spray each green bean with oil and place in air fryer basket. Set temperature to 400 degrees, and air fry for 8 minutes. Shake occasionally, and spray with oil one time during cooking. Remove to a serving bowl and keep warm. Repeat with remaining green beans.

CAJUN FRIED OKRA
with CREAMY CHILI SAUCE
Serves 6 to 8

1 cup	cornmeal
1 cup	all-purpose flour
2 teaspoons	Paula Deen's House Seasoning (see page 40)
¼ teaspoon	Cajun seasoning
½ cup	buttermilk
2 pounds	fresh okra, sliced ½ inch thick
	oil, for spraying

1. In a medium bowl, combine cornmeal, flour, House Seasoning, and Cajun seasoning. Place buttermilk in a small bowl. Dip okra in buttermilk, then dredge in cornmeal mixture. Place on a baking sheet lined with parchment paper. Chill battered okra in refrigerator for 30 minutes.

2. Working in batches of 10, spray okra with oil and place in air fryer basket. Set temperature to 400 degrees, and air fry for 5 minutes. Shake okra well, spray with oil, and air fry for 3 minutes more. Repeat with remaining okra. Serve warm with *Creamy Chili Sauce* on the side.

Creamy Chili Sauce

1 cup mayonnaise
3 tablespoons Thai sweet chili sauce
1 tablespoon garlic chili sauce
⅛ teaspoon ground red pepper

In a small bowl, combine mayonnaise, Thai sweet chili sauce, garlic chili sauce, and red pepper and stir well. Cover and chill until ready to serve.

Makes 1¼ cups

ROASTED BUTTERNUT SQUASH SALAD

Serves 4

1	small butternut squash, peeled, seeded, cut into 1-inch pieces
4 tablespoons	olive oil
1 teaspoon	Paula Deen's House Seasoning (see page 40)
¼ teaspoon	cayenne pepper
2 tablespoons	fresh lemon juice
1	small shallot, minced
¼ teaspoon	salt
6 ounces	arugula
1	small Granny Smith apple, cored and thinly sliced
½ cup	toasted sliced almonds
½ cup	grated Parmesan cheese

1 In a large bowl, combine squash, 2 tablespoons of the olive oil, House Seasoning, and cayenne pepper; toss to coat well.

2 Place squash in air fryer basket, set temperature to 400 degrees, and cook for 15 minutes, shaking occasionally. Let cool.

3 In a large bowl, whisk together lemon juice, shallot, salt, and remaining olive oil. Add arugula and toss to coat. Divide arugula between 4 salad plates and top with squash and apple slices. Sprinkle with sliced almonds and Parmesan cheese. Serve chilled.

CRISPY ZUCCHINI FRIES

Serves 4

½ cup	all-purpose flour
	kosher salt
	freshly ground black pepper
2	eggs
½ cup	panko breadcrumbs
¼ cup	freshly grated Parmesan cheese
½ teaspoon	smoked paprika (optional)
2	zucchini, cut into ½-inch-thick, 4-inch-long slices
	oil, for spraying

1 In a shallow dish, whisk together flour and a large pinch each of salt and pepper. In a second shallow dish, beat together one whole egg and yolk of second egg. Discard extra egg white. In a third shallow dish, whisk together breadcrumbs, Parmesan cheese, paprika (if desired), and a large pinch each of salt and pepper. Dredge zucchini in flour mixture, then dip in beaten egg, and then dredge in breadcrumb mixture.

2 Working in batches, spray zucchini on both sides with oil and place in air fryer basket in a single layer. Set temperature to 400 degrees, and air fry for 5 minutes. Turn zucchini, spray with oil, and air fry for 5 minutes more. Repeat with remaining zucchini.

FRIED SQUASH

Serves 6

½ cup	buttermilk
3	large eggs
4	medium yellow squash, cut into ¼-inch slices
1 cup	yellow cornmeal
1 cup	all-purpose flour
3 tablespoons	Cajun or Creole seasoning
½ cup	baking powder
¼ teaspoon	salt
	freshly ground black pepper to taste
	oil, for spraying
	fresh parsley, chopped, for garnish (optional)

1. In a large bowl, whisk together buttermilk and eggs. Add squash, tossing gently to coat. Let stand for 30 minutes.

2. Drain squash, discarding buttermilk mixture. In a shallow bowl, combine cornmeal, flour, Cajun or Creole seasoning, baking powder, salt, and pepper. Dredge squash in cornmeal mixture and place in a single layer on a baking sheet lined in parchment paper. Spray with oil.

3. Place squash slices oil side down in air fryer basket in a single layer. Do not overcrowd. Spray with oil. Set temperature to 400 degrees, and air fry for 5 minutes. Turn squash, spray with oil, and air fry for 3 minutes more. Remove squash to a serving platter and keep warm. Repeat with remaining squash. Garnish with parsley, if desired. Serve immediately.

BACON-WRAPPED CORN ON THE COB

Serves 4

4 ears corn

8 slices bacon

butter-flavored oil, for spraying

1 Remove husks and silk from corn. Wrap each ear of corn with 2 slices bacon and secure with toothpicks or unwaxed dental floss.

2 In batches of 2, spray bacon-wrapped corn with oil and place in air fryer basket. Set temperature to 375 degrees, and air fry for 10 minutes, or until bacon is browned and cooked through. Turn and spray with oil halfway through cooking. Repeat with remaining corn. Serve warm.

ROASTED BEET SALAD
with COCOA VINAIGRETTE

Serves 2

4	small beets, trimmed and scrubbed
	oil, for spraying
½ teaspoon	salt
½ teaspoon	black pepper
one 5-ounce package	spring mix salad greens
2	oranges, peeled and sectioned
½ cup	walnuts, chopped and toasted
½ cup	goat cheese, crumbled
⅓ cup	thinly sliced red onion
½ cup	cacao nibs

1 Place beets in a shallow bowl, spray with oil, and sprinkle with salt and pepper. Wrap beets in aluminum foil and arrange in air fryer basket. Set temperature to 350 degrees, and cook for 45 minutes. Set foil-wrapped beets aside to cool. When cool, slice and set aside.

2 Evenly divide among 2 salad plates the salad greens, orange sections, walnuts, goat cheese, red onion, and sliced beets. Top each salad with cacao nibs. Drizzle with *Cocoa Vinaigrette* just before serving.

Cocoa Vinaigrette

¼ cup red wine vinegar
1 teaspoon unsweetened cocoa powder
½ teaspoon sugar
salt to taste
freshly ground black pepper
2 tablespoons olive oil

In a small bowl, whisk vinegar, cocoa powder, sugar, salt, and black pepper until smooth. Slowly add oil, whisking constantly until well blended.

SIDES

PARMESAN AND DIJONNAISE-CRUSTED WHOLE CAULIFLOWER

Serves 6

1	large cauliflower	½ teaspoon	freshly ground black pepper
2 tablespoons	Dijon mustard	¼ cup	grated Parmesan cheese
1 tablespoon	mayonnaise		oil, for spraying
1 teaspoon	salt	¼ cup	chopped fresh parsley

1 Remove outer leaves from cauliflower and trim stem flush with bottom of head. In a small bowl, mix mustard and mayonnaise. Cover cauliflower with resulting Dijonnaise. Sprinkle cauliflower with salt and pepper, and press Parmesan cheese into cauliflower.

2 Spray cauliflower with oil and place in air fryer basket. Set temperature to 350 degrees, and air fry for 30 minutes, spraying with oil every 10 minutes. Sprinkle with parsley and serve warm.

SPICY AIR-FRIED GREEN BEANS

Serves 4

½ cup	self-rising flour
½ teaspoon	cayenne pepper
2 teaspoons	chili powder
½ teaspoon	Paula Deen's House Seasoning (see page 40)
2	eggs
½ cup	breadcrumbs
½ pound	green beans, trimmed
	oil, for spraying
	favorite dipping sauce, for serving

1. In a shallow dish, combine flour, cayenne pepper, chili powder, and House Seasoning. In a shallow bowl, beat eggs. Place breadcrumbs in another shallow dish. Roll green beans in flour mixture, shaking off any excess; dip in beaten egg, shaking off excess; and gently roll in breadcrumbs. Place on parchment-lined baking sheet.

2. Working in batches of 10, spray green beans with oil and place in air fryer basket. Set temperature to 400 degrees, and air fry for 4 minutes. Shake basket, spray green beans with oil, and air fry for 5 minutes more. Repeat with remaining beans. Serve warm with your favorite dipping sauce.

FRIED MUSHROOMS

Serves 6

8 ounces	whole mushrooms
¾ cup	all-purpose flour
1 teaspoon	Paula Dean's House Seasoning (see page 40)
2	large eggs
1 cup	breadcrumbs
	oil, for spraying
	favorite dip, for serving

1 With a paper towel, wipe mushrooms clean, then cut tips off stems. In a shallow bowl, mix flour and House Seasoning. In another shallow bowl, beat eggs. Place breadcrumbs in a third shallow bowl. Roll each mushroom in flour, gently shaking off excess; dip in beaten egg, letting excess drip off; and roll in breadcrumbs. Place on a sheet pan for 5 minutes to set up.

2 Working in batches of 8, spray each mushroom with oil and place in air fryer basket. Do not overcrowd. Set temperature to 400 degrees, and air fry for 6 minutes. Turn and spray with oil halfway through cooking. Repeat with remaining mushrooms. Serve warm with a delicious dip.

SIDES

AIR-FRIED ASPARAGUS
with HERBED LEMON AIOLI

Serves 4

2	egg whites
1 cup	panko breadcrumbs
½ cup	Parmesan cheese
½ teaspoon	dried basil
¼ teaspoon	cayenne pepper
1 pound	asparagus, trimmed
	oil, for spraying

1 In a small bowl, lightly beat egg whites. In another small bowl, combine breadcrumbs, Parmesan cheese, basil, and cayenne pepper. Dip asparagus spears in beaten egg whites, then roll in breadcrumb mixture.

2 Working in batches of 10, spray asparagus with oil and place in air fryer basket. Do not overcrowd. Set temperature to 400 degrees, and air fry for 6 minutes. Repeat with remaining spears. Serve warm with *Herbed Lemon Aioli* on the side.

....

Herbed Lemon Aioli

½ cup mayonnaise
1 lemon, juiced
½ tablespoon chopped fresh thyme
½ tablespoon chopped rosemary
¼ teaspoon garlic powder

In a small bowl, combine mayonnaise, lemon juice, thyme, rosemary, and garlic powder. Chill, covered, until ready to use.

CRUNCHY EGGPLANT FRIES

Serves 2

1	large eggplant
1	large egg
2 tablespoons	milk
2 cups	panko breadcrumbs
¼ teaspoon	paprika
1 teaspoon	Paula Deen's House Seasoning (see page 40)
½ cup	shredded Italian cheese blend
	oil, for spraying
	marinara sauce, for dipping

1 Peel eggplant, slice lengthwise into ½-inch slices, and then cut slices into ¼-inch-thick strips. In a shallow dish, beat egg, then whisk in milk. In another shallow dish, combine breadcrumbs, paprika, House Seasoning, and Italian cheese blend. Dip each strip of eggplant in egg mixture, then press into breadcrumb mixture; coat well.

2 Spray each strip of eggplant with oil and place in air fryer basket. Set temperature to 400 degrees, and air fry for 10 minutes. Shake basket and spray eggplant with oil halfway through cooking. Serve warm with warm marinara sauce, for dipping.

CREAMY ROASTED CAULIFLOWER

Serves 2

1 tablespoon	butter
1 tablespoon	olive oil
2 cloves	garlic, minced
1	Vidalia onion, finely chopped
one-half 8-ounce package	cream cheese
¾ cup	heavy cream
1	cauliflower steak, 1 inch thick
	oil, for spraying
	kosher salt to taste
	freshly ground black pepper to taste
1 tablespoon	finely chopped parsley

1. To make creamy cheese sauce, in a medium skillet, melt butter in olive oil over medium–high heat. Add garlic and onion and sauté, stirring occasionally, for 8 minutes, or until onions are soft. Stir in cream cheese and heavy cream and bring to a simmer. Set aside and keep warm.

2. Spray cauliflower steak with oil, and sprinkle both sides with salt and pepper, and place in air fryer basket. Set temperature to 375 degrees, and air fry for 5 minutes. Turn cauliflower steak, spray with oil, and air fry for 3 minutes more. Remove cauliflower steak to a platter, pour cheese sauce on top, sprinkle with parsley, and serve warm.

SIDES

BLUE CHEESE AND BACON BROILED TOMATOES

Serves 2

½ sleeve	round buttery crackers, crushed
1 ounce	blue cheese, crumbled
4 slices	bacon, cooked and crumbled
¼ cup	finely chopped green onion
1 tablespoon	butter, melted
1	large tomato, cut in half crosswise
⅛ teaspoon	salt
⅛ teaspoon	freshly ground black pepper

1. In a small bowl, combine cracker crumbs, blue cheese, bacon, and green onion. Add butter and mix well.

2. Place tomato halves, cut side up, in air fryer basket. Sprinkle tomato halves with salt and pepper. Top each tomato half with half of the cracker mixture. Set temperature to 350 degrees, and cook for 10 minutes, or until lightly browned. Serve warm.

I like to serve these delicious stuffed tomatoes with a salad and turn this side into an entrée.

KALE CHIPS

Serves 2

1 bunch	kale
2 tablespoons	olive oil
1 teaspoon	Paula Deen's House Seasoning (see page 40)
1 tablespoon	grated Parmesan cheese
	oil, for spraying

1. Cut stems off kale, rinse well, and pat dry. In a large bowl, toss kale leaves with olive oil, House Seasoning, and Parmesan cheese, coating thoroughly.

2. Place kale in air fryer basket, set temperature to 350 degrees, and air fry for 10 minutes. Occasionally shake basket and spray kale with oil during cooking.

I just love to keep a batch of these around for snacking.

AN ODE
TO THE POTATO 6

PAULA'S FAVORITES

*Sweet Potato Fries
with Marshmallows* · 153

French Fries · 149

Shepherd's Pie Stuffed Potatoes · 161

SOUTHERN TATER TOTS

Serves 4

2	russet potatoes, peeled
1	egg, beaten
¼ cup	finely minced onions
¼ cup	all-purpose flour
½ teaspoon	cayenne pepper
½ teaspoon	paprika
¼ teaspoon	garlic powder
¼ teaspoon	salt
¼ teaspoon	freshly ground black pepper
	oil, for spraying

1. Using a box grater, finely shred potatoes. Place potatoes in paper towels and squeeze out all excess liquid. Place potatoes on cutting board and finely chop.

2. In a medium bowl, combine potatoes, egg, and onion and mix well. Add flour and stir to combine. Stir in cayenne pepper, paprika, garlic powder, salt, and black pepper. Form potato mixture into tater tots.

3. Working in batches of 10, spray tater tots with oil and place in air fryer basket. Set temperature to 400 degrees, and air fry for 5 minutes. Turn tater tots, spray with oil, and air fry for 4 minutes more, or until golden brown. Remove tater tots to bowl and keep warm. Repeat with remaining tater tots. Serve warm.

HERB BAKED CHEESY POTATOES

Serves 2

2	large russet potatoes, peeled
1 tablespoon	olive oil
1 tablespoon	butter, melted
½ teaspoon	dried rosemary
½ teaspoon	dried thyme
½ teaspoon	salt
¼ teaspoon	freshly ground black pepper
1 cup	Cheddar cheese
½ cup	sour cream
1 tablespoon	chopped chives

1. Slice bottom of each potato along length and lay flat on a cutting board. Carefully cut ⅛-inch slices down potato, three-quarters through, leaving bottom intact.

2. In a small bowl, combine oil and melted butter. Place potatoes in air fryer basket, and brush oil and butter mixture over potatoes and carefully between slices. Sprinkle with rosemary, thyme, salt, and pepper. Set temperature to 375 degrees, and air fry for 35 minutes. Top potatoes with Cheddar cheese, and air fry for 5 minutes more, to melt cheese. Remove potatoes to a platter, top with sour cream, and sprinkle with chives. Serve warm.

DISCO FRIES
Serves 4

Don't get the name? They make you want to get up and dance!

2 tablespoons	butter
¼ cup	finely minced yellow onion
1 cup	beef broth
2 tablespoons	water
1 tablespoon	cornstarch
6	large red potatoes
1	large sweet onion, cut into ½-inch wedges
2 tablespoons	olive oil
	Paula Deen's House Seasoning (see page 40) to taste
2½ cups	shredded Cheddar cheese

1. To make gravy, in a medium saucepan, melt butter. Add minced yellow onion and sauté until tender. Add beef broth and bring to a simmer. In a small bowl, combine water and cornstarch. Add cornstarch to broth, stirring until thickened, about 1 minute. Keep warm.

2. In a large pot, boil potatoes with skins on until almost done. Let cool. Cut potatoes into long strips ¼- to ½-inch thick. In a large mixing bowl, toss sweet onion wedges, cooked potatoes, and olive oil to coat well.

3. Working in batches, place equal portions onions and potatoes in air fryer basket in a single layer. Do not overcrowd. Set temperature to 400 degrees, and air fry for 15 minutes, shaking occasionally. Transfer first batch of onions and fries to a shallow casserole dish, sprinkle with House Seasoning, and keep warm. Repeat with 3 more batches onions and fries, but transfer new batches to a separate bowl.

4. Sprinkle first batch of fries and onions in casserole dish with one-third of the Cheddar cheese. Add two more layers of onions, fries, and cheese. Top with warm gravy and serve immediately.

AN ODE TO
THE POTATO

FRIED POTATOES AND PARSNIPS

Serves 2

1   parsnip, peeled and cut into very thin slices

1   large baking potato, peeled and cut into very thin slices

     oil, for spraying

     sea salt to taste

     black pepper to taste

     fresh parsley, chopped, for garnish

This is a delicious side that complements almost any entrée.

1   Spray vegetables on both sides and place in air fryer basket in a single layer. Do not overcrowd. Sprinkle with salt and pepper. Set temperature to 400 degrees, and air fry for 5 minutes. Turn vegetables, spray with oil, and air fry for 5 minutes more. Repeat with remaining vegetables. Serve garnished with chopped parsley.

SWEET POTATO FRIES

Serves 2

1   sweet potato, peeled and cut into ¾-inch matchsticks

1 tablespoon   extra virgin olive oil

½ teaspoon   kosher salt

½ teaspoon   Cajun seasoning

1 teaspoon   maple syrup

     oil, for spraying

1   In a shallow baking dish, toss potatoes with olive oil, salt, Cajun seasoning, and maple syrup.

2   Lay potatoes in air fryer basket in a single layer. Do not overlap. Spray well with oil. Set temperature to 400 degrees, and air fry for 5 minutes, shaking basket occasionally. Turn potatoes, and air fry for 5 minutes more. Allow fries to cool slightly before serving.

PARMESAN AND GARLIC POTATO CHIPS

Serves 2

2 tablespoons	grated Parmesan cheese
½ teaspoon	garlic powder
¼ teaspoon	minced fresh parsley
¼ teaspoon	black pepper
1	large gold Idaho potato
	oil, for spraying
½ teaspoon	salt

1. In a bowl, mix together Parmesan cheese, garlic powder, parsley, and black pepper.

2. Using a mandoline, slice potato very thin, and soak slices in water to remove starch. Pat potato slices dry with paper towels and place in a single layer in air fryer basket. Set temperature to 350 degrees, and air fry for 5 minutes. Spray potato slices on both sides with oil and sprinkle with salt. Increase temperature to 400 degrees, and air fry for 10 minutes. Shake occasionally, keeping slices in a single layer. Repeat with remaining slices.

3. Place chips in a serving bowl, and toss with Parmesan mixture.

POTATO CROQUETTES

Serves 16

2	large egg yolks
4 cups	cooked mashed potatoes
2 tablespoons	milk
½ teaspoon	chopped green onion
3 tablespoons	flour
1 teaspoon	salt
½ teaspoon	pepper
1 cup	breadcrumbs
	oil, for spraying

1 In a small bowl, beat egg yolks. In a large bowl, combine mashed potatoes, milk, beaten egg yolks, onion, flour, salt, and pepper and mix well. Chill for 1 hour. Place breadcrumbs in a shallow dish. To make each croquette, shape 2 tablespoons of potato mixture into a patty and press into breadcrumbs, covering both sides. Repeat with remaining potato mixture.

2 Working in batches of 6, spray each patty with oil and place in air fryer basket. Set temperature to 400 degrees, and air fry for 10 minutes, shaking basket several times during cooking. Spray with oil at least one time during cooking. Repeat with remaining patties.

FRENCH FRIES

Serves 4

2   russet potatoes, peeled and cut into ¼-inch sticks

oil, for spraying

sea salt to taste

1   In a bowl of ice water, soak cut potatoes for at least 15 minutes. Pat potatoes dry with paper towels.

2   Spray potatoes with oil and place in air fryer basket in a single layer. Do not overcrowd. Set temperature to 320 degrees, and air fry for 10 minutes, to remove moisture. Shake basket, spray potatoes with oil, and sprinkle with salt. Set temperature to 400 degrees, and air fry for 10 minutes, shaking occasionally and adding more oil if you like. Repeat with remaining potatoes.

DEEN FAMILY FRIED BAKED POTATO

Serves 2

1	large russet potato
	oil, for spraying
½ cup	all-purpose flour
1	boneless, thin pork chop
½ cup	Cheddar Jack cheese
2 to 3 tablespoons	cream cheese
¼ cup	bacon bits
	Paula Deen's House Seasoning to taste (see page 40)
	Paula Deen Silly Salt to taste
	butter, melted, for topping

1 Wash potato, spray with oil, and place in air fryer basket. Set temperature to 400 degrees, and air fry for 45 minutes. Remove potato and let cool.

2 Place flour in a shallow dish. Beat pork chop until tender and thin. Dredge pork chop in flour, spray with oil, and place in air fryer basket. Set temperature to 400 degrees, and air fry for 5 minutes.

3 Slice potato in half. Scoop out inside flesh and discard. Cut air-fried pork chop into strips and place in scooped-out potato halves. Add Cheddar Jack cheese, cream cheese, and bacon.

4 Place potato halves in air fryer basket, and air fry for 5 minutes. Sprinkle with House Seasoning and Paula Deen Silly Salt. Serve topped with melted butter.

One of the Deen family's favorite potato and pork chop dishes. This is a twofer.

POTATO AND PANCETTA CAKES

Serves 6

1¾ pounds	potatoes, peeled and rinsed
1 cup	diced pancetta
2 tablespoons	finely chopped onions
2 tablespoons	butter, melted
2	large eggs, beaten
1 tablespoon	milk
2 tablespoons	chopped chives
1 teaspoon	Paula Deen's House Seasoning (see page 40)
4 tablespoons	breadcrumbs
	oil, for spraying

1   In a large saucepan, boil potatoes in salted water until tender. Set aside to cool. When potatoes are cool, chop finely and set aside. In a small sauté pan, cook pancetta for 1 minute. Remove with a slotted spoon and set aside. Pour off all but 1 teaspoon of grease from sauté pan, add onions, and sauté for 1 minute. Add pancetta to onions.

2   In a large bowl, combine potatoes, onion-pancetta mixture, butter, eggs, milk, chives, and House Seasoning.

3   In a 3-inch-diameter ring mold, layer 1 teaspoon of the breadcrumbs followed by 1½ inches of potato mixture. Press down with back of a spoon, and top with 1 teaspoon of the breadcrumbs. Remove mold from around cake, and repeat with remaining potato mixture and breadcrumbs.

4   Working in batches, spray potato cakes with oil and place in air fryer basket in a single layer. Set temperature to 400 degrees, and air fry for 10 minutes, or until golden brown. Turn and spray with oil halfway through cooking. Repeat with remaining potato cakes. Serve warm.

ROSEMARY-GARLIC POTATO WEDGES

Serves 4

4	Yukon Gold potatoes, cut into wedges (or fingerlings)
3 cloves	garlic, minced
1 sprig	rosemary, leaves removed and chopped fine
1 teaspoon	Paula Deen's House Seasoning (see page 40)
1 teaspoon	lemon juice
¼ teaspoon	cayenne pepper
1 tablespoon	grated Parmesan cheese

1. In a large bowl, toss all ingredients well. Marinade for 20 minutes, tossing occasionally.

2. Place half of the potatoes in air fryer basket, set temperature to 400 degrees, and air fry for 12 minutes. Shake basket and spray potatoes with oil halfway through cooking. Repeat with remaining potatoes and serve warm.

ROASTED SWEET POTATOES AND RED POTATOES

Serves 2

½ cup	diced sweet potatoes
½ cup	diced red potatoes
	oil, for spraying
	salt to taste
	freshly ground black pepper to taste

1. In a small bowl, combine sweet potatoes and red potatoes. Spray potatoes with oil and sprinkle with salt and black pepper. Place potatoes in air fryer basket, set temperature to 375 degrees, and air fry for 30 minutes, shaking occasionally. Serve warm.

SWEET POTATO FRIES
with MARSHMALLOWS
Serves 2

2 tablespoons	coconut oil
1 teaspoon	salt
½ teaspoon	cayenne pepper
1 cup	cornstarch
1 cup	club soda (must be cold)
2	sweet potatoes, peeled and cut into ¼-inch fries
	oil, for spraying
½ cup	miniature marshmallows

1. In a large bowl, blend coconut oil, salt, and cayenne pepper. In another large bowl, stir cornstarch in cold club soda until dissolved. Add sweet potatoes and toss to coat well. On a rack, drain potatoes of excess coating.

2. Place half of the potatoes in air fryer basket and spray with oil. Set temperature to 400 degrees, and air fry for 10 minutes, shaking occasionally. Toss fries in coconut oil mixture and return to air fryer basket. Air fry for 10 minutes, or until golden brown. Place fries on a baking sheet, and place in a warm oven. Repeat with remaining fries.

3. After all fries are cooked, place in air fryer basket, add marshmallows, and toss. Air fry for 5 minutes, shaking occasionally. Serve warm.

AIR-FRIED BAKED POTATO SKINS

Serves 4

2	russet potatoes
	oil, for spraying
1 tablespoon	Paula Deen's House Seasoning (see page 40)
1 cup	shredded Cheddar cheese
6 slices	bacon, cooked crisp and crumbled
1 cup	sour cream
2 tablespoons	horseradish
4 tablespoons	sliced green onion
½ cup	chopped tomato
2 tablespoons	chopped chives

1 Scrub potatoes and pat dry. Spray potatoes with oil and sprinkle with House Seasoning. Place potatoes in air fryer basket, set temperature to 400 degrees, and cook for 40 minutes. Remove potatoes and set aside to cool.

2 When cool, cut potatoes in half lengthwise and scoop out interior flesh, leaving a ¼-inch shell. Discard flesh or reserve for another use. Spray potato skins with oil and place in air fryer basket. Set temperature to 400 degrees, and air fry for 5 minutes, or until golden brown. Fill each potato skin with Cheddar cheese and bacon, spray with oil, and air fry for 5 minutes more.

3 In a small bowl, combine sour cream and horseradish. Top cheese-filled potato skins with green onion, tomato, and sour cream–horseradish sauce. Garnish with chives.

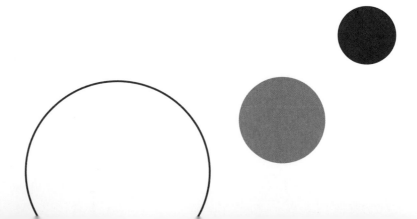

BOBBY'S LIGHTER SPICY SHRIMP-STUFFED POTATOES

Serves 2

1	large russet potato
	oil, for spraying
¼ cup	reduced-fat sour cream
2	canned mild green chiles, chopped
⅛ teaspoon	salt, plus more to taste
6	medium shrimp, peeled and deveined
1 teaspoon	chili powder
½ teaspoon	olive oil
¼ cup	reduced-fat shredded Cheddar cheese
2 tablespoons	chopped fresh cilantro

1. Wash and dry potato and gently prick with a fork. Spray potato with oil and place in air fryer basket. Set temperature to 375 degrees, and cook for 45 minutes. When potato is cool, cut in half lengthwise. Scoop interior flesh into a medium bowl, leaving two ½-inch-thick skins.

2. In a medium bowl, mash potato flesh with sour cream, chiles, and ⅛ teaspoon of the salt until coarsely mashed.

3. Spray a medium nonstick skillet with nonstick spray. Add shrimp and cook over medium-high heat, turning occasionally, until shrimp are opaque, about 3 minutes. Transfer to a cutting board, let cool slightly, then coarsely chop.

4. In a medium bowl, toss shrimp with chili powder, olive oil, and pinch of salt. Stir chopped shrimp into potato mixture until well combined.

5. Stuff potato shells with shrimp mixture and top each with half of the Cheddar cheese. Place potatoes in air fryer basket, set temperature to 375 degrees, and air fry for 7 minutes, or until browned on top. Sprinkle with cilantro before serving.

BACON TURKEY POTATO TOWERS

Serves 2

2	medium russet potatoes
	oil, for spraying
2 teaspoons	Paula Deen's House Seasoning (see page 40)
1 cup	sour cream
1 teaspoon	smoked paprika
½ cup	chopped deli turkey
¾ cup	shredded Cheddar cheese
2	slices bacon
½ cup	Paula Deen barbecue sauce
4	green onions, sliced thin, for garnish

1. Spray potatoes with oil and sprinkle all over with ½ teaspoon of the House Seasoning. Place potatoes in air fryer basket. Set temperature to 350 degrees, and cook for 45 minutes. Set aside to cool. When potatoes are cool, cut a small portion from bottom of each potato. Turn each potato over and slice off top. Scoop out potato flesh and discard or save for another use.

2. In a small bowl, combine sour cream, paprika, and remaining House Seasoning. Stuff each potato with turkey and cheese layers, beginning with turkey and ending with cheese on top. Wrap each potato with bacon slice and secure with toothpicks.

3. Place potato towers in air fryer basket. Set temperature to 400 degrees, and air fry for 10 minutes, basting with Paula Deen barbecue sauce halfway through cooking. Sprinkle with green onions and serve warm.

PARMESAN-CRUSTED POTATO ROUNDS

Serves 6

6	medium new red potatoes
	oil, for spraying
4 tablespoons	grated Parmesan cheese
1 teaspoon	Paula Deen's House Seasoning (see page 40)
¼ cup	butter, melted

1. Spray potatoes with oil and place in air fryer basket. Set temperature to 350 degrees, and cook for 45 minutes. Set aside to cool. When potatoes are cool, cut into ¼-inch-thick slices.

2. In a shallow bowl, combine Parmesan cheese and House Seasoning. Pour melted butter in another small bowl. Dip potato slices in butter and press into Parmesan mixture to coat both sides.

3. Working in batches, spray potato slices with oil, and place in air fryer basket in a single layer. Set temperature to 400 degrees, and air fry for 6 minutes. Turn and spray with oil halfway through cooking. Repeat with remaining potatoes and serve warm.

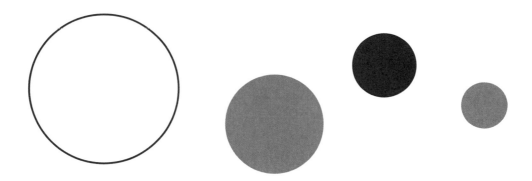

STUFFED BREAKFAST POTATO

Serves 2

2	medium russet potatoes
	oil, for spraying
1 teaspoon	Paula Deen's House Seasoning (see page 40)
2 tablespoons	shredded Cheddar cheese
2	large eggs
4 slices	bacon, cooked crisp and crumbled, for garnish
2	green onions, finely sliced, for garnish

1 Spray potatoes with oil, sprinkle with House Seasoning, and place in air fryer basket. Set temperature to 350 degrees, and cook for 45 minutes. Set aside to cool. When potatoes are cool, cut a small portion from bottom of each potato. Turn each potato over and slice off top. Scoop out two-thirds of the potato flesh and discard or save for another use.

2 To each potato, add 1 tablespoon of the Cheddar cheese, and crack one egg into each potato. Place in air fryer basket, and cook for 5 minutes, or until egg whites are set and yolks are runny. Sprinkle with crumbled bacon and green onions.

SHEPHERD'S PIE
STUFFED POTATOES

Serves 2

1	small onion, diced
1 tablespoon	extra-virgin olive oil
2 tablespoons	brown gravy mix
4 tablespoons	water
1 cup	cubed leftover roast beef
1	large russet potato
	oil, for spraying
	Paula Deen's House Seasoning (see page 40) to taste
¼ cup	milk
2 tablespoons	butter, room temperature
¼ teaspoon	salt
¼ teaspoon	black pepper
4 tablespoons	canned corn (or peas)
2 tablespoons	shredded Cheddar cheese

1 In a skillet over medium heat, sauté onions in olive oil until slightly browned. Add gravy mix and water, mix well, and simmer until thickened. Add roast beef, cook for 1 minute, and set aside.

2 Spray potato with oil, sprinkle with House Seasoning, and place in air fryer basket. Set temperature to 350 degrees, and cook for 45 minutes. When cool, cut potato in half lengthwise and scoop out interior flesh into a medium bowl, leaving a ¼-inch shell.

3 To potato flesh, add milk, butter, salt, and black pepper. Using a hand mixer, blend until smooth. Divide roast beef mixture between each potato half, followed by 2 tablespoons corn in each. Spoon or pipe potato mixture into skins.

4 Sprinkle each potato half with Cheddar cheese and place in air fryer basket. Set temperature to 400 degrees, and air fry for 5 minutes, or until heated through and cheese is light brown. Serve warm.

MASHED POTATO EGG ROLLS

Serves 6

2 cups	mashed potatoes
8	slices bacon, cooked crisp and crumbled
4	green onions, sliced
1	egg
1 teaspoon	Paula Deen's House Seasoning (see page 40)
8	cheese sticks, 3 inches long
8	egg roll wrappers
	oil, for spraying

1. In a medium bowl, combine mashed potatoes, bacon, green onions, egg, and House Seasoning; mix well. Mold 3 tablespoons potato mixture around each cheese stick, completely covering cheese, to form a log.

2. Place one egg roll wrapper on a flat surface with one corner pointing toward you. Using a pastry brush, lightly brush corners with water. Place potato log in center of egg roll wrapper. Roll bottom corner of wrapper over log, fold left and right corners over log, and tightly roll toward remaining corner, pressing gently to seal. Repeat with remaining egg roll wrappers and potato logs.

3. Working in batches of 4, spray egg rolls with oil and place in air fryer basket. Set temperature to 400 degrees, and air fry for 8 minutes. Turn and spray with oil halfway through cooking. Repeat with remaining egg rolls and serve warm.

SWEET POTATO AND BACON TATER TOTS

Serves 4

2	large sweet potatoes
2 slices	bacon, cooked and crumbled
3½ tablespoons	all-purpose flour
½ teaspoon	salt
	oil, for spraying

1. In a pot, boil sweet potatoes until partially done, about 15 minutes. Drain and let cool. When cool, using a box grater, shred potatoes. Squeeze potatoes in paper towels to remove all moisture—the most important step to prepare a perfect tater tot.

2. In a medium bowl, combine potatoes, bacon, flour, and salt; mix well. Form 1 tablespoon of the potato mixture into one tater tot. Repeat with remaining potato mixture.

3. Working in batches of 6, spray tater tots with oil and place in air fryer basket. Set temperature to 400 degrees, and air fry for 12 minutes. Turn and spray with oil halfway through cooking. Repeat with remaining tots and serve warm.

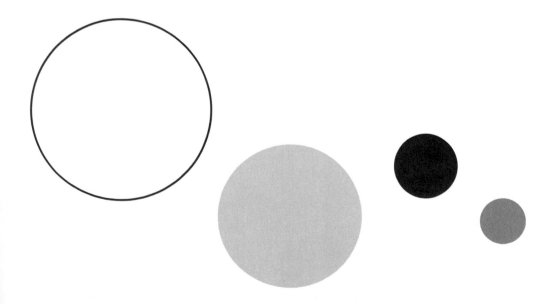

TEX-MEX TWICE-BAKED SWEET POTATO

Serves 2

1	large sweet potato
	oil, for spraying
1 teaspoon	Paula Deen's House Seasoning (see page 40)
2	jalapeño peppers, seeded and chopped
¼ cup	chopped onion
4 slices	bacon, cooked and crumbled, 1 tablespoon grease reserved
2 tablespoons	sour cream
2 tablespoons	shredded Mexican-style four-cheese blend
2	green onions, sliced, for garnish
	salsa, for serving

1 Spray sweet potato with oil, sprinkle with House Seasoning, and place in air fryer basket. Set temperature to 350 degrees, and cook for 45 minutes. When cool, cut potato in half lengthwise and scoop out flesh into a medium bowl, leaving two ¼-inch shells.

2 In a small sauté pan, sauté jalapeño peppers and onion in reserved bacon grease over medium heat for 2 minutes. In a small bowl, combine jalapeño-onion mixture, crumbled bacon, sweet potato flesh, and sour cream; mix well.

3 Spoon half of the potato mixture into each potato skin and top with cheese blend. Place potato halves in air fryer basket, and air fry for 5 minutes, or until heated through and cheese is melted. Garnish with green onions and serve with your favorite salsa.

STUFFED SWEET POTATOES

Serves 2

1	large sweet potato	2 teaspoons	maple syrup
	oil, for spraying	⅛ teaspoon	nutmeg
2 tablespoons	brown sugar	¼ teaspoon	ground ginger
2 tablespoons	unsalted butter	1 cup	miniature marshmallows

1 Spray sweet potato with oil and place in air fryer basket. Set temperature to 350 degrees, and cook for 45 minutes. When cool, cut potato in half lengthwise and scoop out flesh into a medium bowl, leaving two ¼-inch-thick shells.

2 To the sweet potato flesh, add brown sugar, butter, maple syrup, nutmeg, and ginger, and using a hand mixer, blend well.

3 Fill potato skins with sweet potato mixture and top with marshmallows. Set temperature to 400 degrees, and air fry for 5 minutes, or until marshmallows are golden brown.

ROASTED RED POTATOES
with MUSTARD VINAIGRETTE

Serves 2

2 tablespoons	olive oil
½ tablespoon	grainy mustard
½ tablespoon	white wine vinegar
1 tablespoon	roughly chopped parsley
1	shallot, finely chopped
	salt to taste
	black pepper to taste
1 cup	diced new red potatoes
	oil, for spraying
2 cloves	garlic, peeled and crushed

1. To make vinaigrette, in a small bowl, whisk together olive oil, mustard, vinegar, parsley, shallot, salt, and black pepper.

2. In a small bowl, spray potatoes with oil, add garlic, toss to coat, and sprinkle with salt and black pepper. Place potatoes in air fryer basket, set temperature to 375 degrees, and cook for 30 minutes, or until tender and golden brown, shaking occasionally. Toss hot potatoes and vinaigrette and serve warm.

PAULA'S FAVORITES

FRIED BISCUITS
—FOR EASY DONUTS

Yields 8 donuts

one 12-ounce can   buttermilk biscuits

oil, for spraying

cinnamon sugar

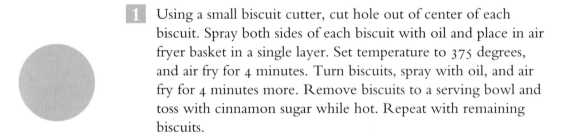

1   Using a small biscuit cutter, cut hole out of center of each biscuit. Spray both sides of each biscuit with oil and place in air fryer basket in a single layer. Set temperature to 375 degrees, and air fry for 4 minutes. Turn biscuits, spray with oil, and air fry for 4 minutes more. Remove biscuits to a serving bowl and toss with cinnamon sugar while hot. Repeat with remaining biscuits.

AIR-FRIED OREOS

Serves 8

one 12-ounce can   refrigerated crescent dough

8   Oreo cookies

oil, for spraying

1   Separate dough triangles. Wrap each dough triangle around one Oreo, completely encasing cookie. Press dough to seal.

2   Working in batches of 4, spray each Oreo with oil and place in a single layer in air fryer basket lined in parchment paper. Set temperature to 350 degrees, and air fry for 5 minutes. Turn Oreos, spray with oil, and air fry for 3 minutes more, or until golden brown. Repeat with remaining Oreos. Serve warm or cold.

NUTELLA AND BANANA–STUFFED FRENCH TOAST *with* CORN FLAKE CRUST

Serves 4

2	large eggs
⅓ cup	whole milk
3 teaspoons	granulated sugar
¼ teaspoon	ground nutmeg
¼ teaspoon	salt
1½ cups	crumbled corn flakes
4	slices challah (2 inches thick), preferably a few days old
4 tablespoons	Nutella
2	ripe bananas, peeled and sliced into 16 rounds
	oil, for spraying
	powdered sugar, for dusting (optional)
	cocoa powder, for dusting (optional)

1. In a small bowl, beat eggs. In a shallow dish, mix milk, beaten egg, granulated sugar, nutmeg, and salt. Place corn flakes in a shallow dish.

2. Cut a slit in top crust of each bread slice. Using a spoon, stuff each bread slice with 1 tablespoon of the Nutella, followed by 4 slices of the banana. Dip each bread slice in egg mixture until entirely covered. Press each bread slice into corn flakes and coat both sides.

3. Working in batches of 2, spray stuffed bread slices with oil and place in air fryer basket. Set temperature to 400 degrees, and air fry for 8 minutes. Repeat with remaining slices. Serve hot, dusted with powdered sugar or cocoa powder, if desired.

AIR-FRIED CANNOLI

Yields 12 cannoli

⅔ cup	heavy cream
⅓ cup	powdered sugar, plus more for dusting
1 cup	ricotta cheese
3 tablespoons	amaretto
1 teaspoon	ground cinnamon
¼ cup	chopped unsalted pistachios
3	8 × 10-inch or larger fresh pasta sheets
	oil, for spraying
½ cup	miniature chocolate chips

1. In a food processor, whip cream while slowly adding powdered sugar until soft peaks form. Place ricotta cheese in a large bowl, and whisk in amaretto and cinnamon. Stir half of the whipped cream into ricotta cheese mixture. Gently fold in remaining whipped cream, and then gently fold in pistachios. Fill a pastry bag with no tip with ricotta cheese mixture.

2. Cut pasta sheets into twelve 4-inch circles. Spray cannoli forms with oil, then wrap pasta sheets around forms. Seal edges together with water–dipped fingertips.

3. Working in batches of 4, place cannoli forms in air fryer and spray with oil. Set temperature to 400 degrees, and air fry for 5 minutes. Turn cannoli forms, and air fry for 2 minutes more. Remove cannoli forms from air fryer, and using tongs, slide out forms while cannoli shells are still hot. Repeat with remaining pasta circles. If reusing forms, allow to cool before preparing each batch.

4. Pipe filling into air-fried cannoli shells just up to the edges. Dip each end of cannoli into miniature chocolate chips and dust with powdered sugar before serving.

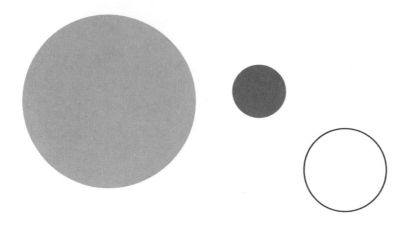

AIR-FRIED
BUTTER FINGERS

Serves 12

one 16-ounce box	powdered sugar
1 cup (2 sticks)	butter
1 teaspoon	vanilla extract
2½ cups	all-purpose flour
¾ cup	granulated sugar
	oil, for spraying

1. Place powdered sugar in a medium bowl. In a food processor, combine butter, vanilla extract, flour, and granulated sugar. Roll butter mixture into small "fingers."

2. Working in batches of 4 to 6, spray butter fingers with oil and place in air fryer basket. Do not overcrowd. Set temperature to 350 degrees, and air fry for 5 minutes, or until desired brownness. Remove to a platter and dredge immediately in powdered sugar. Repeat with remaining butter fingers.

A finger-lickin'. butterly delicious recipe.

AIR-FRIED
CHERRY-WALNUT PIES

Yields 12 pies

⅔ cup	light corn syrup
⅓ cup	butter, melted
2	large eggs, plus 1 egg yolk, beaten
1 cup	granulated sugar
1½ cups	chopped walnuts
1 teaspoon	vanilla extract
⅛ teaspoon	salt
½ cup	finely chopped dried cherries
	flour, for dusting
two 15-ounce packages	refrigerated pie crust (found in dairy section)
	oil, for spraying
	powdered sugar, for dusting

1 In a cold saucepan, combine corn syrup, melted butter, 2 eggs, and granulated sugar. Stir in walnuts, vanilla extract, and salt and bring to a boil over medium heat. Reduce heat and simmer for 10 minutes. Stir in cherries and let cool for 20 minutes.

2 On a lightly floured surface, unroll 1 pie crust. Using a biscuit cutter, cut 4-inch-diameter circles in dough. Combine dough scraps, roll out, and cut more circles. Stack dough circles between wax paper. Repeat with remaining pie crust.

3 On a flat surface, lightly brush edges of one circle with beaten egg yolk. Place 1 heaping tablespoon of the walnut mixture in center of circle. Fold dough over filling, pressing edges to seal. Repeat with remaining circles.

4 Working in batches of 2, spray both sides of pies with oil and place in air fryer basket. Set temperature to 400 degrees, and air fry for 5 minutes. Turn pies, spray with oil, and air fry for 3 minutes more. Remove pies to a platter and immediately dust lightly with powdered sugar. Repeat with remaining pies.

FRIED APPLE PIES

Serves 8

2 tablespoons	butter
4	McIntosh apples, peeled, cored, and sliced
½ cup	granulated sugar
½ teaspoon	ground cinnamon
1 teaspoon	lemon juice
	flour, for dusting
one 8-biscuit package	refrigerated jumbo flaky biscuits
	oil, for spraying
	powdered sugar, for dusting

1. To make filling, in a large sauté pan, melt butter. Add apples, granulated sugar, cinnamon, and lemon juice. Sauté over medium heat until apples are soft, about 15 minutes. Remove from heat and cool.

2. On a lightly floured surface, roll out biscuits into 7- to 8-inch–diameter circles. Place 2 or 3 tablespoons of the apple filling on each circle and brush edges with water. Fold half of each circle over filling to make a half-moon shape. Seal by pressing edges with tines of a fork.

3. Working in batches of 2, spray pies on both sides with oil and place in air fryer basket lined with parchment paper. Set temperature to 350 degrees, and air fry for 5 minutes. Flip pies, spray with oil, and air fry for 5 minutes more. Repeat with remaining pies. Dust pies with powdered sugar.

For quick and easy pies, use one 21-ounce can apple pie filling instead of making your own.

SWEETS

AIR-FRIED STRAWBERRIES

Yields 8 strawberries

8	large strawberries, washed and patted dry
4 teaspoons	honey-flavored cream cheese
one 8-ounce package	crescent dinner rolls
	oil, for spraying
	powdered sugar, for dusting

1 Slice each strawberry in half lengthwise, leaving stem and leaves intact. Fill each strawberry half with ½ teaspoon cream cheese, and rejoin the two halves. Wrap each strawberry with one triangle of crescent dough, leaving stem and leaves exposed. Pinch edges of dough to seal.

2 Working in batches of 4, spray dough–wrapped strawberries with oil and place in air fryer basket. Set temperature to 400 degrees, and air fry for 4 minutes. Turn strawberries, spray with oil, and air fry for 4 minutes more. Remove strawberries to a serving dish and immediately dust with powdered sugar. Repeat with remaining strawberries.

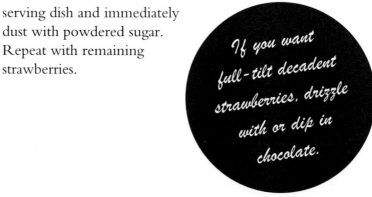

If you want full-tilt decadent strawberries, drizzle with or dip in chocolate.

AIR FRYER S'MORES
Serves 4

1	egg
¼ cup	milk
4	large egg roll wrappers
½ cup	prepared chocolate frosting
8	regular-size marshmallows
½ cup	graham cracker crumbs
	oil, for spraying
4 tablespoons	fudge sauce
	powdered sugar, for dusting

1 To make an egg wash, in a small bowl, beat egg, then whisk in milk.

2 Lay one egg roll wrapper on a flat surface, and place 2 tablespoons of the chocolate frosting in center of wrapper. Top wrapper with 2 marshmallows. Moisten edges of wrapper with egg wash. Fold top of wrapper down over marshmallows, and fold both sides toward center. Roll marshmallow packet toward you until completely rolled up, making sure roll is tightly packed and edges sealed. Repeat with remaining wrappers, frosting, and marshmallows.

3 Place graham cracker crumbs in a medium bowl. Using a pastry brush, coat rolls with egg wash, then gently roll in graham cracker crumbs.

4 Spray each roll on all sides with oil and place in air fryer basket. Set temperature to 400 degrees, and air fry for 5 minutes. Turn rolls, spray with oil, and air fry for 5 minutes more. Remove S'mores to serving dish, drizzle with fudge sauce, and dust with powdered sugar. Serve hot.

ULTIMATE FANTASY AIR-FRIED CHEESECAKE

Serves 8

1 cup	graham cracker crumbs	8	spring roll wrappers
1¼ cups	granulated sugar	2 ounces	semi-sweet chocolate, chopped
7 teaspoons	butter, melted	¼ cup	fresh raspberries
three 8-ounce packages	cream cheese, softened		powdered sugar, for dusting
5	eggs		oil, for spraying
one 4-ounce bar	white chocolate, melted and cooled slightly		chocolate sauce, for topping
			whipped cream, for topping
1 tablespoon	milk	8 sprigs	fresh mint, for garnish

1. To make the cheesecake, preheat oven to 350 degrees. In a medium bowl, using a wooden spoon, combine graham cracker crumbs, ¼ cup of the granulated sugar, and melted butter. Press mixture firmly into the bottom and 1 inch up the sides of a 9-inch springform pan. Bake for 8 minutes until crust becomes slightly golden.

2. Using an electric mixer, in a large bowl, beat cream cheese and 1 cup of the granulated sugar until fluffy. Add 4 of the eggs, one at a time, and beat until mixture becomes light, about 3 minutes. Stir in white chocolate. Carefully pour batter into graham cracker crust and bake for 45 minutes. Let cool completely on a wire rack, then chill for 8 hours. Cut cheesecake into 8 equal pieces and freeze before using.

Instead of baking a cheesecake, you may substitute a 9-inch cheesecake from your local bakery and freeze it before preparing for air-frying.

SWEETS

3   To make an egg wash, whisk remaining egg with milk. Using a pastry brush, lightly brush spring roll wrappers with egg wash, blotting off excess with paper towels. Place one piece of frozen cheesecake in the center of each wrapper and sprinkle with chopped chocolate and raspberries. Fold spring roll wrapper over top of cheesecake, bringing both sides toward the center. Roll each piece of cheesecake toward you until completely encased, making sure roll is tightly packed and edges are sealed. Place powdered sugar in a medium bowl.

4   Working in batches of 4, spray each roll with oil and place in air fryer basket. Set temperature to 400 degrees, and air fry for 5 minutes. Turn rolls, spray with oil, and air fry for 5 minutes more. Remove each roll and immediately coat well with powdered sugar. Repeat with remaining rolls.

5   Before serving, drizzle with chocolate sauce, top with whipped cream, and garnish with mint.

SWEETS

BAKED APPLES

Serves 2

1 cup	firmly packed brown sugar
½ cup	raisins
1 teaspoon	ground cinnamon
½ cup (1 stick)	butter, room temperature
6	large Honey Crisp or Gala apples, cored
	butter-flavored oil, for spraying

1. In a small bowl, combine brown sugar, raisins, cinnamon, and butter; mix well.

2. Spoon sugar butter into center of each apple. In batches of 3, spray apples with oil and place in air fryer basket. Set temperature to 350 degrees, and cook for 20 minutes. Repeat with remaining apples. Serve warm.

PAULA'S CHOCOLATE CHIP OATMEAL COOKIES

Makes 24 cookies

1½ cups	all-purpose flour
1 teaspoon	baking soda
½ teaspoon	salt
1 cup (2 sticks)	unsalted butter, room temperature
¾ cup	packed brown sugar
¾ cup	granulated sugar
2	large eggs
1 teaspoon	vanilla extract
½ teaspoon	water
2 cups	quick-cooking rolled oats
2 cups	chocolate chips
1 cup	toasted chopped pecans (optional)

The dough for these tasty cookies can be made ahead of time and stored in a ziplock freezer bag for up to 6 months.

1   Place baking pan in air fryer, set temperature to 400 degrees, and preheat for 10 minutes.

2   In a medium bowl, whisk together flour, baking soda, and salt. In a large bowl, using a hand mixer, cream butter, brown sugar, and granulated sugar until fluffy. Add eggs, one at a time, and mix until fully incorporated. Add vanilla extract and water, and beat until fully incorporated. Add flour mixture to butter mixture and mix well. Stir in oats and chocolate chips. Add nuts, if desired.

3   In batches of 4, place 2 tablespoons dough into air fryer baking pan. Set temperature to 320 degrees, and cook for 10 minutes. Repeat with remaining dough, or make as many cookies as you like.

CINNAMON-SUGAR PECANS

Serves 4

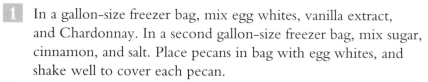

2	large egg whites
½ tablespoon	vanilla extract
1 tablespoon	Chardonnay
1 cup	sugar
1 tablespoon	ground cinnamon
½ teaspoon	salt
1 pound	pecan halves

1. In a gallon-size freezer bag, mix egg whites, vanilla extract, and Chardonnay. In a second gallon-size freezer bag, mix sugar, cinnamon, and salt. Place pecans in bag with egg whites, and shake well to cover each pecan.

2. Place half of the pecans in sugar mixture. Shake well to cover each pecan. Line bottom of air fryer basket with parchment paper, and place sugar-coated pecans in basket in a single layer. Set temperature to 250 degrees, and air fry for 30 minutes. Shake basket every 5 minutes. Repeat with remaining pecans. Let pecans cool before serving.

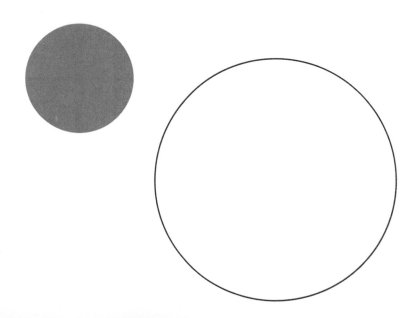

FRIED PEACH PIE

Serves 4

	flour, for dusting
one 8-ounce package	crescent dinner rolls
4 tablespoons	peach pie filling
	oil, for spraying
¼ cup	prepared vanilla frosting

1. On a lightly floured flat work surface, lay out 4 crescent roll triangles. Place 1 tablespoon of the peach pie filling in center of each triangle and cover with remaining 4 crescent roll triangles. Crimp edges with a fork to seal.

2. Working in batches of 2, spray both sides of pies with oil and place in air fryer basket. Set temperature to 400 degrees, and air fry for 5 minutes. Turn pies, spray with oil, and air fry for 5 minutes more. Remove pies to a serving platter. Repeat with remaining pies.

3. In a small microwave-safe bowl, microwave frosting for 25 seconds. Drizzle pies with warm frosting.

CINNAMON-SUGAR DONUT STICKS

Serves 4

one 12.4-ounce can	cinnamon roll dough
	oil, for spraying
1 teaspoon	granulated sugar
1 teaspoon	ground cinnamon

1 On a flat surface, separate dough into rolls, flatten each roll, and cut each into 3 strips. Roll each strip lengthwise into tight sticks.

2 Working in batches of 4, spray each dough stick with oil and place in air fryer basket in a single layer. Set temperature to 350 degrees, and air fry for 4 minutes. Turn donut sticks, spray with oil, and air fry for 3 minutes more. Remove to a plate and keep warm. Repeat with remaining dough sticks.

3 In a medium bowl, blend sugar and cinnamon, add donut sticks, and toss. Drizzle with cinnamon roll icing and serve warm.

FRENCH-BREAD DESSERT SANDWICHES

Serves 4

8 slices	French bread, 1 inch thick
4 tablespoons	marshmallow creme
4 tablespoons	chocolate-hazelnut spread
2	bananas, sliced into rounds
	butter-flavored oil, for spraying
	powdered sugar, for dusting

1 Spread one side of 4 of the French bread slices with 1 tablespoon of the marshmallow creme. Spread one side of remaining bread slices with 1 tablespoon of the chocolate-hazelnut spread and top with sliced bananas. Place marshmallow creme bread slices on top of chocolate-hazelnut slices to make sandwiches.

2 Working in batches of 2, spray both sides of sandwiches with oil and place in air fryer basket. Set temperature to 350 degrees, and air fry for 3 minutes. Turn sandwiches, spray with oil, and air fry for 3 minutes more. Remove sandwiches to a serving tray and keep warm. Repeat with remaining sandwiches. Dust with powdered sugar and serve immediately.

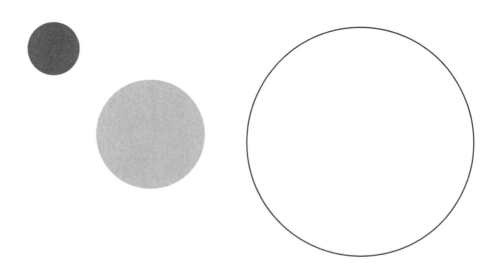

FRIED CANDY BARS

Serves 8

one 12-ounce can	refrigerated crescent dough
8	miniature candy bars, chilled in refrigerator
	oil, for spraying
½ cup	powdered sugar

1. Separate dough triangles, and wrap each triangle around one candy bar.

2. Working in batches of 4, spray wrapped candy bars with oil and place in air fryer basket. Set temperature to 375 degrees, and air fry for 5 minutes. Turn candy bars, spray with oil, and air fry for 2 minutes more, or until golden brown. Remove candy bars to a platter and immediately sprinkle with powdered sugar. Repeat with remaining candy bars. Serve warm.

SWEETS

BANANA-NUTELLA EGG ROLLS

Serves 8

1	large banana
8	egg roll wrappers
6 ounces	Nutella, 2 ounces reserved for drizzling
	oil, for spraying
4 tablespoons	powdered sugar

1. Peel banana, cut in half lengthwise, and cut again in fourths to create 8 pieces.

2. Place one egg roll wrapper on a flat surface with one corner pointing toward you. Using a pastry brush, lightly brush corners with water. Spoon ½ ounce of the Nutella in center of egg roll wrapper. Place one piece of the banana horizontally in middle of wrapper. Fold bottom corner of wrapper over banana. Fold left and right corners over banana. Tightly roll filled end toward remaining corner, pressing gently to seal. Repeat with remaining egg roll wrappers.

3. Working in batches of 2, spray egg rolls with oil and place in air fryer basket. Set temperature to 400 degrees, and air fry for 10 minutes. Turn and spray with oil halfway through cooking. Repeat with remaining egg rolls.

4. In a small microwave-safe bowl, heat remaining Nutella for 15 seconds, or until thin enough to pour. Sprinkle egg rolls with powdered sugar and drizzle with warm Nutella. Serve warm.

SWEETS

189

MAPLE-GLAZED BACON DONUTS

Serves 8

one 12-ounce can	refrigerated biscuit dough
½ cup	prepared vanilla frosting
½ teaspoon	maple extract
4 slices	bacon, cooked and crumbled
	oil, for spraying

1. Using a small biscuit cutter, cut hole out of center of each biscuit to form donuts. In a small microwave-safe bowl, microwave vanilla frosting for 30 seconds. Add maple extract and mix well. Place crumbled bacon in a shallow dish.

2. Working in batches of 2, spray donuts with oil and place in air fryer basket. Set temperature to 375 degrees and air fry for 4 minutes. Turn, spray with oil, and air fry for 4 minutes more.

3. While hot, dip top of each donut in maple glaze and then in bacon. Place on a wire rack. Repeat with remaining donuts.

AIR-FRIED POP TARTS

Serves 4

2	eggs
1 teaspoon	water
	flour, for dusting
one 15-ounce package	refrigerated pie crust (found in dairy section)
¾ cup	strawberry preserves
	oil, for spraying
1 cup	powdered sugar
1½ tablespoons	milk
½ teaspoon	vanilla extract
1 tablespoon	candy sprinkles, for garnish

1. To make egg wash, in a small bowl, whisk eggs and water.

2. On a lightly floured surface, unroll pie crusts and separate. Cut each into four 3 × 2-inch rectangles, yielding 8 rectangles. Spread strawberry preserves in center of 4 rectangles, leaving ¼-inch border on all sides. Cover with remaining 4 dough rectangles and press edges with a fork to seal. Brush pop tarts with egg wash.

3. Working in batches of 2, spray each pop tart with oil, and place in the air fryer basket lined with parchment paper. Set temperature to 350 degrees, and air fry for 10 minutes. Repeat with remaining pop tarts.

4. To make glaze, in a small bowl, combine powdered sugar, milk, and vanilla extract. Drizzle pop tarts with glaze, and sprinkle with candy sprinkles. Serve warm.

PEACHES AND CREAM–STUFFED FRENCH TOAST

Serves 2

4 ounces	whipped cream cheese
1 teaspoon	sugar
½ teaspoon	fresh lemon juice
4	large eggs
½ cup	milk
¼ teaspoon	ground cinnamon
4 slices	challah bread, 2 inches thick
12	fresh peach slices (or frozen, thawed)
	oil, for spraying
¼ cup	powdered sugar, for dusting

1. To make filling, in a small bowl, combine cream cheese, sugar, and lemon juice; set aside. In a medium shallow bowl, beat eggs, then stir in milk and cinnamon. Place bread slices in egg mixture and soak for 5 minutes, turning once.

2. Cut a slit in top crust of each bread slice. Using a spoon, stuff each slice with one-quarter of the cream-cheese filling and 3 peach slices.

3. Working in batches of 2, spray stuffed bread slices with oil and place in air fryer basket. Set temperature to 350 degrees, and air fry for 10 minutes. Turn halfway through cooking. Repeat with remaining sandwiches. Dust with powdered sugar and serve warm.

FOUR-LAYER BUTTER CAKE
with CHOCOLATE FROSTING

Serves 8

one 16-ounce box	yellow cake mix
4	large eggs
1 cup	buttermilk
1 teaspoon	vanilla extract
⅓ cup	unsalted butter, room temperature
	nonstick baking spray
16 ounces	prepared chocolate fudge frosting

1. Set air fryer temperature to 400 degrees, and preheat for 10 minutes.

2. In a large bowl, combine cake mix, eggs, buttermilk, vanilla extract, and butter. Using a hand mixer on low, mix for 1 minute. Increase speed to high, and mix for 3 minutes more.

3. Spray 6-inch diameter spring form pan with nonstick baking spray. Pour half of the cake batter into pan, and place in air fryer. Set temperature to 320 degrees, and cook for 30 minutes. Test for doneness: if wooden skewer inserted in middle of cake comes out clean, cake is done. If not cooked through, cook for 5 minutes more. Let cake rest several minutes, then invert onto a plate, and then invert cake again.

4. Spray spring form pan with nonstick baking spray, and repeat with remaining cake batter.

5. Let cakes cool for 1 hour. You may freeze slightly before torting. Cut top off of each cake to level, then cut each cake into two layers. Start by tracing line around middle of one cake with a long serrated knife. Then slowly rotate cake, following that line with the knife cutting toward the center. After a few rotations, cake will be sliced in two. Repeat with remaining cake.

6. Frost each layer, sides, and top of cake with your favorite chocolate fudge frosting.

INDEX OF RECIPES